What's Wrong With Your Small Business Team?

Leander Jackie Grogan

groganbooks.com

Publishing Services Worldwide

Business Edition - Hardback

Copyright © 2012 by Leander Jackie Grogan

All rights reserved.

Visit website at: www.antheadsystem.com

Printed in the United States of America
Second Printing: January, 2012
ISBN-978-1-61364-033-3

Dedication

This book is dedicated to my devoted family and ever-believing friends who have been so supportive over the years; and to Goggle Search which made life so much easier and reminded me of how far we've come from those microfilm canisters and "get-on-the-waiting list--check-out-the-book" library days. I also want to remember the many small business owners ... Percy Creuzot, Hazel Obey, Robert Kramer, Sonceria Messiah-Jiles, Earl Nash, Alfred White, Debbie Warner, Anthony Newton, Rufus Conley and so many others ... who trusted me enough to allow me to look behind the scenes of their fragile operations so that I might contribute to their success. To all of you who didn't die from the stress of making payroll or over-indulgence in those after-hours Jack Daniels business mixers, I salute you. May God bless your tireless, tenacious, innovative souls.

About the Author

Leander Jackie Grogan's excellence in writing extends over a multiplicity of genres. Grogan is a graduate of Texas Tech University, Business Technology Masters student and twenty-year veteran in the marketing, management and communications industries. A perennial college commencement, Chamber of Commerce and Lyons Club speaker, he has been recognized in Houston Business Journal's WHO"S WHO IN HOUSTON series and The City of Houston/ Guaranty Federal Bank Business Person of the Month Awards. He ran a small business for fourteen years and served as a strategic consultant to many small business operations.

He has won numerous local and national awards including the Silver Microphone National Award, Houston Association of Radio Broadcasters Award, Matrix Award and Crystal Communicator Award of Excellence and has authored a number of nonfiction articles in such national magazines as *Houston Business, AdWeek, Black Enterprise and Jet*. He has also written numerous business articles for online business magazines and national blogs.

In the world of fiction, his books have been distributed in eleven countries and in five different languages. View more at: www.antheadsystem.com.

TABLE OF CONTENTS

Preface

From *The Death of Management: Restoring Value to the U.S. Economy by Jack Buffington, to Leadership And Project Management: Time For A Shift From Fayol To Flores* by Gregory A. Howell, Hal Macomber, Lauri Koskela and John Draper, to the *Wall Street Journal's Essential Guide To Management* by Alan Murray, the ominous warning is the same: After years of driving companies into the ground, management, as we've known it in the past, is dead ... or on nonfunctional life-support, desperately waiting for the replacement model to arrive.

In this book, we discuss one of the replacement models, an innovative, groundbreaking system especially designed for small businesses ranging from startup infancy to five-year-old proactive expansion. Under this new system, the road will be bumpy. The traditional entrepreneur will be challenged and stretched in ways never imagined. The small business owner will have to become a nimble sky-walker with an array of leadership styles and expansive knowledge of managing ambiguities, personal preferences and case by case scenarios. He or she will have to find solid footing in the quicksand of uncertainly and seize each moment of opportunity as though it will never come again. Because, in all likelihood, in this volatile, ever-evolving economy, it won't come again.

Strap in for the roller-coaster ride of your life designed to catapult you to the next level of business operations. Examine for yourself the evolutionary small business model everyone's talking about ... The Anthead Syndrome.

CHAPTER

1

The Journey Begins

*W*e begin this journey with a hypothetical scenario. You're driving to a convention in Dallas or Phoenix or Pensacola. You've brought along your top sales representative, let's call him Big Mike, and left your other eight employees back at the office with specific tasks to complete.

A hundred miles down the highway, you delve into the business at hand, the real reason you wanted him to accompany you to the event. Big Mike seems to understand the true essence of your product line. He's aggressive, takes care of his customers (your customers) and is responsible for generating 55% of all sales, with the other two salespeople equally splitting the remaining 45%. You realize, as you grow, you're going to need a competent sales manager, someone who can organize, supervise and motivate the sales department to reach new heights in the ever-evolving landscape of business opportunities.

But Big Mike doesn't seem interested in motivating, cooperating or assisting his cohorts. In fact, in previous conversations, he's made subtle remarks indicating he considers them to be deadbeats.

11

You say: I notice you don't talk much to Sally and Wayne (the other two salespeople). Is there a reason for that?

Mike says: I feel like if I'm going to hit my numbers, I can't really waste a lot of time chewing the fat.

You say: Well, I'm not sure we can characterize every conversation with them as chewing the fat. Sometimes they reach out to you for help. They see your success rate. They want to know what you're doing so they can improve too.

Mike says: If I spend all my time trying to tell them how to do their job, then I won't have time to do mine.

You say: Yes, Mike. But we're a team. We've got to help each other. That's the only way we'll grow in the future.

Mike says: At the end of the month, when we look at the numbers, there's no category on the spread sheet for helping. You hired me to move product and that's what I do.

Needless to say, you're very disappointed, perhaps, even furious. You're tempted to turn around, take him back to the office, give him his final check and send him on his way. You don't need selfish people in your organization. You need team players, people who will bond together for the common good, right? How can you build a tightly integrated organization when people are only out for themselves? In the back of your mind, you're already developing a strategy to replace him with someone who will fit the team mode.

Now, I ask the question: Who's right? You or Big Mike?

This might surprise you. But Big Mike is right. I warned you in the Preface it was going to be a bumpy ride.

The fuzzy logic behind Mike's position is a bit entangled and convoluted. So let's begin with the simplest component of his improbable defense: *incentification*.

What incentives have you incorporated into your organizational procedures to reward people for *helping*? What tangible effort have you made to place value on individual performance and behavior related to the act of assisting and mentoring others?

Being a small business or startup operation, the answer is probably none. Yet, leading corporations make a practice of rewarding company-endorsed behavior. General Electric (GE), for instance, has built-in incentives designed to recognize employees who go out of their way to assist others. Google, which values employees going (environmentally) green, offers free, tasty organic gourmet meals, use of plug-ins for hybrid vehicles and discounts to employees who install solar equipment at home. Bank of America offers a reimbursement of $3,000 to employees purchasing a new hybrid vehicle. Hitchcock Chairs in Connecticut has a value-based awards program called *You're A Star*, where employees nominate fellow employees who are caught "doing things in the spirit of the company."

What these companies are saying is, "We encourage certain values and behaviors, and are willing to put our money where our mouth is." What are you saying to Big Mike? Maybe, you're saying, "Do it because I'm your boss, I sign your check and I want you to do it."

Secondly, because you are a small business entrepreneur and not a Harvard psychology major, you may not be aware of Big Mike's profile, or where he fits in the overall scheme of things. With all of the other responsibilities of running a company, I wish I could tell you it's not important that you delve into the analytical world of human profiling. But it *is* important. In building a superior small business team, you're going to have to know your team members from head to toe.

According to Lancaster and Stillman, authors of *Generations Collide: Who They Are. Why They Clash. How to Solve the Generational Puzzle at Work,* there are four distinct generational career categories:

- Traditionalists
- Baby Boomers
- Generation Xers
- Millennials (also Linksters)

A brief examination of each category will help you to better understand why Big Mike has responded in such a detached, uncooperative manner.

Generational Employee Types

Traditionalists

Traditionalists are generally older, loyal, dependable workers who put aside personal gains for universal goals. They've been shaped by the Great Depression and World Wars, and are accustomed to sacrificing for the common good. They have simple career goals, predominately, to be accepted as valuable contributors to the work group, provide a decent living for their families and retire with enough money in the bank to live comfortably, and perhaps, take a few vacations now and then. Envision President Jimmy Carter, without his political affluence, working in your organization. He commands a wealth of valuable knowledge that books can't teach and is accustomed to doing things a certain way ... methodically and efficiently, without the slightest deviation.

Baby Boomers

Baby Boomers are creatures in search of balance. They were born in the late forties to early sixties, never touched a computer in high school, remember the Cuban missile crisis, witnessed the 1960's civil rights movement, remember the introduction of birth control pills, lost confidence in Democracy during the Nixon scandals, and naively believed that a college degree was the cure for all ills. They seek recognition and face-time with the boss, search for meaning in life outside of the company, live and die by the television, and are very competitive due to the large number of people in their generation versus the available jobs. In many instances, having to answer to a younger boss, they feel overlooked and undervalued for their steadfast contribution and the knowledge they possess. They live in a perpetual world of "fearful" forced transformation where new technologies and processes seem to conspire to keep them one step behind.

Generation Xers

Generation Xers, the so-called unknown generation, born after 1961, are perpetual skeptics, impacted by the high divorce rates, urban violence and the explosion in new technology. They've watched the failure of many respected institutions and grand schemes such as the War on Drugs, Safe and Secure US Borders and the promise of energy independence. They dislike authority and rigid work requirements. Experiencing the rise of video games and the internet, they are extremely resourceful and independent thinkers. They could care less about face-time with the boss or interaction with coworkers. They prefer an isolated work environment with transparent parameters and goal-oriented instructions.

Millennials

Millennials, also known as Generation Y, and Linksters, born 1978-2000 and the children of Baby Boomers, are overly realistic, absorbed by the internet, masters of digital communications, used to a global economy, driven by the language of market efficiency and consumer choice. They are the most tech-savvy, most eco-conscious generation in America. They like to collaborate with their peers and are loyal as long as it's convenient. A recent survey of over two hundred job recruiters classified Millennials as poor performers in need of an attitude adjustment. Some managers refer to Millennials as the *"oh, yeah"* generation, meaning when discussing their lack of initiative and pointing out tasks they've left incomplete, they say, "oh, yeah." (I didn't think of that.)

In their book, *Generations, Inc. From Boomers to Linksters-Managing the Friction Between Generations at Work*, Larry Johnson and Meagan Johnson, a popular father-daughter consulting team, refer to teenagers still living at home and working part-time as Linksters. The name is derived from their status as a generation linked-up and connected since birth. The internet, Facebook and Twitter were always an intricate part of their social existence. They cannot imagine a world without the social media tools that allow them to collaborate instantaneously. It's a natural phenomenon for them to choose speed over thoroughness and dread work environments that move too cautiously or methodically. And for reasons not altogether logical, Linksters are perpetually upbeat and express a strong sense of optimism about their careers, with almost total disregard for the statistics associated with the current economic downturn and a scarcity of jobs.

When we examine these profiles, we quickly realized Big Mike, who's only twenty-eight years old, is not a Great Depression, World War II traditionalist. And yet, the basis on which you tried to persuade him to change his behavior was best suited for the traditionalist generation. It's worth a private hoot to imagine how disconnected your appeal for his investment in the common good must have sounded.

Generation Xers are more "me-right-now" individuals. It's not to say they're more malicious or unfeeling than previous generations. It simply means their brains are wired differently. Unlike Baby Boomers, they aren't driven by the broad "Peace Corp" reforms their actions might have on society. Indicative of the guy who created the computer Love Virus; Onel de Guzman didn't consider the billions in damages his actions would cause. Rather, it was all about establishing himself as a legendary master programmer among his peers.

Since you now know Big Mike is an Xer and (until you replace him) a vital contributor to your business, let's look a bit closer at his characteristics.

We should begin by accepting the fact that he is a perpetual skeptic. Victimized by downsizing and layoffs, Wall Street fraud and government complicity, and the fall from grace of many of his potential heroes (Bill Clinton, Madonna, Newt Gingrich, Herman Cain, Roger Clemens, Michael Vick and others), he harbors a deep distrust, not only for companies and institutions, but leaders who claim to have seen the light and know the way. It may come as a surprise, but you fall into that latter category. You're saying, "I'm the captain of this ship, and I see a bright future if we work together and help each other as a cohesive unit."

There's nothing wrong with that statement. As a visionary, you're supposed to be optimistic and forward-thinking, ultimately, giving hope to the masses and leading with bold direction into the perilous future. But optimism as a closing argument has no value to Big Mike. He's heard it all before. Furthermore, the future of which you speak may or may not be a bed of roses for him. How many entrepreneurs do you know that never share the wealth with employees? They drive into the parking lot in their BMW one day, their Navigator the next, and on their MTT Turbine Superbike motorcycle the next. Then, at the weekly meeting, while punching numbers into their brand new $800 Blackberry, they explain why salaries will have to be cut and people will have to be laid off.

Most Xers see themselves as a self-motivated, self-contained, non-institutionalized *guns-to-hire*. They want to do a good job, get handsomely paid and be left alone. This attitude is as much a protective mechanism or protection filter as it is a dubious perspective on the state of corrupt corporate America. They're saying, "The less I trust you and allow myself to get personally and emotionally involved, the less you can hurt me when the Enron-polluted sky comes crashing down ... again."

Big Mike's perspective is not an illusion. In 1978, CEOs at the helm of major corporations earned 35 times as much as the average worker. In 2009, that gap had grown to 300 times as much. According to economist Edward N. Wolff at New York University, the wealthiest 10% of Americans earned 50% of all income, twelve times as much as the bottom 10%. The top 10% owned 80% of all stocks, bonds, trust funds, and business equity, and over 75% of non-home real estate.

In a starker comparison of income distribution for 2010, the wealthiest .01% earned 6% of all income, owned 35% of all privately held wealth and paid a lower tax rate than 20% of earners just below them, a greater disparity than during the Roaring Twenties.

Meanwhile, the middle class continues to shrink with seventeen million college-educated Americans unable to find jobs commensurate with their educational levels, suburban middle class families, experiencing a 53% increase in poverty, and job cuts and mandatory reductions in weekly hours forcing one in four Americans to apply for emergency food assistance.

Big Mike and other Xers have watched this scenario play out for years. In an unencumbered capitalistic system that rewards executives billions in bonuses for driving their bailed-out companies into the ground, while simultaneously laying off lower level workers in order to cut costs, we should not be surprised to discover capitalism, in its purest form, is not a system Xers trust. Your company is smaller, but still a product of the system, and for all practical purposes, a replica of the ingrained privileged upper class/deprived lower class mentality that market-driven economies facilitate. The rich accuse the middle and lower classes of being frivolous, of not wanting to work and sacrifice. The middle and lower classes accuse the rich of buying laws and lawmakers, exploiting special privileges and loopholes, and perpetuating a systematically stacked deck handed down to them by their rich fathers and grandfathers.

Tea Party Patriots and Wall Street protesters stir the media pot each day with charges, counter-charges and an array of new statistics that keep the conduct of American businesses in the forefront. Thus, being a small business doesn't let you off the hook. In fact, small companies with a single owner and no Board of Directors to serve in a governance capacity are notorious for abusing both employees and customers on a smaller scale, and then disappearing into the dark of night.

Then, there's the sleazy side of the system that, week after week, radiates throughout the media in lime green colored headlines, serving as a reminder that getting ahead is not always the result of fair play and hard work.

Over the last few years, preparing to write this book, I've collected a sprinkling of media clips that attest to the continuing erosion, on a grand scale, of American business ethics. This is not to imply that all the apples in the capitalistic bushel have gone bad. But no one will deny that each year, the percentage of bad apples continues to increase.

Citigroup Inc. and JP Morgan Chase & Co., the largest and second largest US banks respectively, reached an agreement with the Securities and Exchange Commission (SEC) to pay a combined $255 million in fines in connection with their involvement in the fraud perpetrated by Enron.

The US Justice Department charged JGC Corp. Houston with one count of conspiracy and one count of aiding and abetting violations of the Foreign Corruption Practice Act. JGC agreed to pay $218.8 million and criminal penalties to avoid prosecution.

Garrett Bauer of New York and Matthew Kluger of Oakton, VA have been charged with multiple counts of insider trading and obstruction in addition to single counts of conspiracy and money laundering.

Former U.S. House Majority Leader Tom DeLay, once considered among the nation's most powerful and feared lawmakers, was sentenced to three years in prison Monday for a scheme to influence elections that already cost him his job, leadership post and millions of dollars in legal fees.

Two former computer programmers at convicted Ponzi-scheme operator Bernard Madoff's firm were indicted on charges they allegedly helped Mr. Madoff hide a massive fraud from regulators. The three-count indictment charges Jerome O'Hara and George Perez with conspiracy, falsifying the books and records of a broker-dealer and investment adviser.

An executive at a West Deptford cardboard-box manufacturer was found guilty yesterday by a federal court jury of making more than $40,000 in payoffs to Philadelphia union leader Harry Benn to obtain favorable labor contracts. Michael Sarbello, an owner of Associated Packaging Co. Inc., faces up to 100 years in prison and $1 million in fines under federal racketeering laws.

Galleon Group LLC billionaire co-founder Raj Rajaratnam, at the center of the largest US crackdown on hedge-fund insider trading, is accused of gaining $63.8 million from tips leaked by corporate insiders and hedge-fund traders about a dozen stocks.

A 45-year-old Dallas man has pleaded guilty to one count of mail fraud, acknowledging he raised about $7 million in investor funds under false pretenses. In a scheme that began in 2008, Alan Todd May falsely claimed to own and operate oil and gas leases in Texas, Oklahoma, Colorado and Arkansas. May took money from over 170 investors.

European Union regulators fined consumer products companies Procter & Gamble and Unilever for fixing prices of powdered laundry detergent together with Henkel in eight EU countries.

Doris Vinitski, owner of a Houston-area durable medical equipment (DME) company, was sentenced to 84 months in prison for her role in a Medicare health care fraud scheme involving more than $2 million in false billings.

Three years after taxpayers footed the bill to bail out mortgage giants Fannie Mae and Freddie Mac, the top six executives at the government-supported lenders were charged by the Securities and Exchange Commission with fraud for failing to disclose billions of dollars in risky subprime mortgages.

The list goes on with hundreds of cases each year that go unprosecuted.

As we remove our rose-tinted glasses and look at the business arena through the eyes of Big Mike and other Xers, the task of diffusing their suspicions and convincing them to climb aboard our little "promise-to-be-different" gravy train becomes a frightening proposition. And yet, that is precisely what we must do. We must hone in on the one, indispensable component necessary to develop a winning team flush with Xers. That component is *trust*.

Trust

Trust is a relatively simple concept. It hinges on whether a person genuinely believes in the stated intentions, principles, and objectives of an individual or group of individuals. It's a state of interaction where confidence supersedes fear. Notice; fear is not absent from the equation, but rather, suppressed by a greater sense of confidence. Trust is what Southwest Airlines and Ben & Jerry's have; an underlying belief that the company is going to do the right thing.

Here's the great irony in all of this. Big Mike doesn't trust you and you've done nothing to deserve it. But now that you have a basic understanding of how Xers perceive the world and how they're driven by "events of betrayal" unrelated to your actions, you know not to take it personally.

So how do you get Big Mike and other Xers to trust you?

Ughh. Why do you have to ask such hard questions this early in the book? Is it because you're a young, hard-driving entrepreneur with a thousand irons in the fire? Or, is it because you, too, are a "me-right-now" Generation Xer who expects immediate results? Either way, I won't take your impatience personally. Why don't we jump right in?

How do you get Xers to trust? It begins with an open, up-front, in-person verbal request. (Not email or Facebook or iPhone texting!)

You say: I've noticed your exceptional performance. I appreciate all you've been doing. I feel you have a bright future here, and given the opportunity, can offer a great deal more to this company. But you need to know I'm going to treat you right. From this point on, I'm going to make a conscientious effort to win your confidence and trust so that as you take on more responsibility, there is no doubt in your mind the short-term and long-term benefits and rewards will be there for you. Would you be willing to open up and give me a chance to earn your confidence in me as well as this company?

Your exact words will probably be different. But the components must be the same. Express your appreciation for his current contribution to the organization. Let him know he's important enough for you to have spent some time thinking about his future. Reaffirm the potential for him to grow and prosper. Let him know this is a new beginning with a specific objective in mind. Put him on guard to watch your actions and determine whether you are different from other leaders who have disappointed him. Confirm that he is willing to take down some of his pre-deployed protection filters and give you a chance from this point forward.

In future chapters, I will talk more about Appreciative Inquiry. But for now you should know it is an organizational development system introduced in the 1980's by David Cooperrider and Suresh Srivastva. Appreciative Inquiry or *AI* is based on the assumption that an organization changes in the way it inquires or frames the questions of change, and if an organization inquires exclusively into problems or difficult situations, it will keep finding more of the same. But an organization that tries to appreciate what is best in itself (best people, best practices, and best future outcomes) will discover what is best about itself.

The beautiful thing about the concept is that it drills down to one-on-one interactions between managers and subordinates within the organization. The inquiry should be: appreciative, applicable, provocative, and collaborative. And the questions should be designed to foster positive relationships and builds on the basic goodness in a person which helps him or her to envision a positive future.

Isn't that what you're accomplishing in the above statement; showing appreciation, initiating a positive relationship, and giving the Xer an opportunity to envision a positive future?

Here's another thing you should notice about the statement. It invites the Xer to be a mutual collaborator within the process. It says, "watch me." It implies the Xers' observation and judgment is important. It also elicits rather than demands an opportunity to perform for him.

This is a far cry from the old command-structure management system Traditionalists used doing the industrial revolution (Do it because I said do it). This command-structure management system, often referred to as the *command and control* management model, was first introduced in the early 1900's by Henri Foyol, a French mining engineer who organized and embellished the foundation of management theory based on revolutionary new concepts such as sophisticated forecasting, centralized planning, unifying and harmonizing productivity and tracking against specific standards. More importantly, the act of motivating and controlling worker was defined as a top-down dictatorship based on incentives or punishment. Workers who followed orders were rewarded with jobs for life.

Baby Boomers successfully extended the life of this system until the late 70's when women and minorities entered the work-force in droves and forced a new way of thinking. Still, many companies tried to hold on to the old system for the sake of its familiarity and control.

With Xers, and now Millennials, holding critical positions within the organization, the command-structure military form of management is almost extinct. Dictatorial management supremacy over employees is being replaced by *leader-employee* partnerships in which leaders are more like coaches and less like bosses.

Building trust with today's employees in this volatile marketplace is a huge challenge and completely different, by the way, from proving who's right or wrong. Remember how you were ready to take Big Mike back to the office and send him on his way because he was ... wrong?

Some small business owners spend an inordinate amount of time trying to show employees how "wrong" or "off base" they are so they'll be reluctant to question the owner's judgment in the future. This is totally counterproductive to your company's growth and creates an atmosphere of compliance and a team of *yes-men/yes-women* whose contributions are stymied by overriding thoughts of self-preservation. They agree with you because they want to keep their jobs. In Chapter Two, I'll explain how this *yes-men/yes-women* environment contributes to a fast ride down the tubes.

Polarity Management

In gaining the trust of your team, you have to employ a practice known as polarity management. It's a popular problem-solving model that recognizes the existence of more than one right answer. In the traditional approach to problem-solving, there is one right answer. We say, $2 + 2 = 4$, or the United States has 50 states. These equations contain one right answer. Conversely, with polarity management, equations may contain two or more right answers.

How do I get from Texas to the California? The answer to this question produces more than one right answer. If you focus on the mode of transportation, you could drive or fly. If you look at the highway system leading the California, there are many roads that ultimately get you to your destination. The key to successful polarity management is acknowledging the existence of multiple options and choosing the best combination of options that meet stated objectives.

Said another way, in gaining the trust of employees, business owners must go into each exchange open to the possibility that their solution may not be the best one. This is scary territory because it pushes the owner down a road of non-assumptive questioning which is critical in encouraging employees to share new ideas. It also forces the owner to separate the act of receiving information from the act of making a premature judgment on its value.

Ever talked to a superior who couldn't hear what you were saying because she was so busy preparing her rebuttable? Her objective was not to resolve the issue with the most effective solution. Her objective was to reach a conclusion that supported her preconceived position.

Here's what you hope your team will say about you: "My boss is not afraid to listen. And if you show him a better way, he's willing to try it." This is one of the highest compliments a manager can receive.

Gaining trust also has to do with consistency of judgment. That may seem contrary to the flexible sky-walker approach I described earlier, but it's not. It's very important to understand the key to consistency of judgment is communications.

Let's say since Becky, normally a reliable team member, had her baby, she's always late. She overstays her lunch trying to catch up on lost sleep, and quite often, asks to get off a half hour early so she can pick up her child at the nursery. Let's say Monica stays late on Wednesday night getting a presentation ready for a critical meeting scheduled for that following Thursday morning.

Now, let's say both Becky and Monica walk in together Thursday morning. They're both late. You call Becky in and give her a written warning, but you say nothing to Monica. Unless you communicate the basis for your decision, it might appear you're picking on Becky and showing favoritism toward Monica. In this situation your response is different to the same violation. But your judgment is consistent.

Some owners would say, "It's my company. I don't owe an explanation to anyone."

With this attitude you'll never build trust or a powerful team. Remember, in the new dynamics of team building, you are as much accountable to your employees as they are to you.

> **You say:** Becky, your skills are excellent and your contribution is appreciated. So it's important to me you understand the situation. You've been getting a lot of breaks because you have a new baby. But I feel you're beginning to take advantage of my kindness. And if you're wondering about Monica, do you think it's fair for Monica, who stayed here until 10 p.m. last night preparing a presentation, to be denied the same consideration you've received because she doesn't have a child? Each employee has earned a certain amount of discretion. But yours has gone too far.

This puts an end to the behind-the-scenes grumbling and potential discord before it can get started.

"My boss tries to be fair to everybody." That's what you expect from this scenario. And if Becky doesn't express that sentiment to other team members, this is one employee you do need to send on her way.

According to the Bureau of Labor Statistics, between 2007 and 2011, 589,000 incorporated small businesses disappeared. Most successful small business owners who are still around in such a volatile marketplace have had to come to terms with certain sobering realities. Specifically, many owners have come to realize stagnant rules and walls of compliance are cripplers in this new hyperactive marketplace. As the primary manager, owners have been forced to adapt to an array of diverse pressures, requiring spontaneous, customizable solutions. One day you're unable to fill product orders because a just-in-time inventory plane went down in Brazil. The next day you have one key employee making sexual harassment allegations against another. The next day your internet mall store is down again and your largest customer decides to place his orders with a manufacturer offshore. Let's face it. *This ain't your father's old Oldsmobile.* It's a whole new ball game.

That's why it's so critical to develop a solid business team to combat these simultaneous, ever-expanding obstacles to your company's success. You cannot accomplish this task without establishing a foundation of trust.

It's important to understand that trust is not based on only perceived good intentions, but competency as well. In other words, no matter how pure your intentions are, if you consistently fail to achieve your stated objectives, your team will eventually become afraid to follow you.

From their vantage point, they are taking a calculated risk. They are wagering their well-being, and perhaps, the well-being of their families, on the proposition that you will make good decisions, grow the company, and make payroll every two weeks. If your leadership is consistently riddled with mistakes, your team loses trust; not in your intentions, but in your ability to deliver.

In the British Parliament, a vote of no-confidence is a motion traditionally put before the governing members by the opposition party in hopes of exposing the standing government's weaknesses and ineffectiveness. If the no-confidence motion carries, the standing government must respond in one of two ways: either resign or seek new general elections.

Back in 2007, failing to meet expectations of its Trustees,

Hershey's entire Board of Directors (with the exception of two members) had to resign. In 2010, after the BP oil spill, CEO Tony Hayward had to resign because stakeholders lost confidence in his ability to lead the company through the crisis.

It's your company. So no one's going to ask you to resign. Instead, your employee will do it for you, one by one, until all of your key players are gone. What a waste in training and investment of your time.

Of course, being competent doesn't mean being perfect. You're going to make mistakes. Mistakes, however, can offer an additional opportunity to gain the trust of your team members if you're willing to admit to them and make the necessary adjustments. Just make sure you don't have to admit too many.

Transparency offers another opportunity to build trust, especially among Millennials who are well versed in market efficiencies and value chains. A value chain, first introduced by Michael Porter in his book, *Competitive Advantage: Creating and Sustaining Superior Performance*, is a summary of all the support activities in the process of creating and disturbing a product or service to the end-user. The chain is indicative of a grape that turns into a raisin that turns into a mincemeat pie. Activities that add value are documented along the way.

Examination of a value chain can show whether the raisin came from Australia, Chile, Colombia, or maybe China where sweat shops and child labor are responsible for your very low price. Invariably, it tells the story of how far a company is willing to go to make a profit.

Nike, Reebok, and Kathie Lee Gifford's line of clothing sold to Wal-Mart are just a few examples of how the use of unethical manufacturing practices such as sweatshops and child labor can damage a brand and pull valuable resources (time, money, strategic expertise) away from the core operations to address unprofitable damage control activities.

McDonald's was inadvertently pulled into a costly, brand-damaging scandal when Starzen, a Japanese meat packing company, confessed to a long history of mixing cheap meats with more expensive ones and selling the product at a premium price. Texaco was hit with a class action lawsuit by thirty thousand Ecuadorians for allegedly polluting the Amazon, allowing billions of gallons of oil to spill, and leaving hundreds of tar pits unlined and uncovered. Imperial Sugar was summoned before Congress, fined million of dollars and cited for sixty-one egregious, willful violations with plain indifference to employee safety and health, when it's refinery in Port Wentworth, Georgia blew up, killing thirteen and injuring dozens more.

"Ah-hah!" says the Xer to the rest of the team. "I knew this company was rotten to the core."

Transparency is good ... as long as it's good for you. But when it exposes undesirable practices, it's a major deterrent to gaining trust. The lesson is clear. Don't engage in business practices you cannot afford to have come to the light. Don't gouge your customers or get your financing from the Mafia or invest in offshore projects with Enron. If you do, don't use transparency as a vehicle for building trust.

Reciprocal Trust

Finally, and often controversial in many business circles, reciprocal trust is another means by which you may foster trust among your employees. Reciprocal trust is a fancy way of saying if I trust you, maybe you'll reciprocate and trust me too. In its infancy, reciprocate trust meant as long as you performed well at your current job, you could count on continued employment, and ultimately, a nice retirement pension at the end. This is no longer true.

The context of reciprocal trust has been constricted to apply to real time inaction between managers and subordinates, or in your case, entrepreneurs and their employees. The down-and-dirty truth is large corporations hire to meet specific needs. When the needs are gone, the *needs-meeters* are let go.

In 2009, when Pfizer purchased Wyeth and Merck purchased Schering-Plough, the consolidations resulted in 60,000 pharmaceutical and biotech workers losing their jobs. In the past eighteen months, because of the growth in netbooks powered by the Linux operating system, Microsoft has laid off 5,000 people, with the probability of more to come. Borders trimmed thousands of employees trying, unsuccessfully, to stay afloat. In 2011, Gannett Company cut its workforce by 2% worldwide. AT&T handed out pink slips to 12,000 workers, while Credit Suisse handed out another 5,300.

Companies are scrambling to cut costs and reduce their head count. But in a ruthless, dog-eat-dog economy, this is a practice you don't want to follow. As we discuss this in more detail in Chapter Two, you will see how not following this layoff policy and investing in the longevity and stability of your employees will give you a (HubSpot style) strategic advantage in the marketplace.

With regard to the contemporary use of reciprocal trust, how many times have you attended a meeting and heard upper management say, "Now, we trust you to act responsibly on this" or "No one's watching you, but we expect that you will police yourselves and do the right thing ... blah, blah, blah". What she's really saying is the IT logs show some of you are spending the whole day on Facebook, and if you don't stop, we're going to block access to the internet including Facebook, Twitter, YouTube and all your favorite porn sites.

The controversial side of this reciprocal trust approach is the difficulty of implementing and verifying compliance with the policy. In simple terms, if you give your employees the option to do the right thing, how can you tell whether they're doing the right thing unless you verify. And, if you find a few bad apples neither following policy nor honoring their end of the bargain, do you change the policy or institute new policies to weed them out? And how much energy are you willing to expend verifying and weeding?

> **You say:** Okay, salespeople. You may take the company car home on the weekends. But if you fill it up on Friday afternoon and submit that charge on your expensive account, you need to bring it back on full Monday morning, meaning you pay for any gas you might use over the weekend. Don't bring the car back on empty Monday morning and then fill up on company time and expect the company to reimburse you for it.

What happens when one or two bad apples start to violate the policy? Do you institute a new policy? Or do you just stop salespeople from taking company cars home on the weekend?

Your extension of good faith can easily backfire and turn into a negative trust factor. My personal preference would not be to discontinue the program, but rather, have the salespeople check each other on Monday morning and sign off on a form that states falsification can lead to immediate termination. That way, the other salespeople, fearful of losing their privileges, force the bad apple to comply.

Managers on the extreme end of reciprocal trust declare the whole process is a waste of time. Their approach is to set the policy and then reward or punish accordingly. They feel the declaration of trust is superfluous if you're going to verify and then take action based on what you've found.

This extreme approach actually makes good sense. But what the extremists fail to recognize is the power of perceived intent. By employing reciprocal trust policies, the team perceives that, at every opportunity, you are looking out for their best interest. It's a small gesture, but indicative of your commitment to their well-being. How can they not trust an owner with that attitude? And if they mess things up for themselves, they have no one else to blame.

In this chapter, we've spent a great deal of time developing a strategy to gain Big Mike's trust; and rightly so. With effective team building, trust is the foundation for all other strategies. And since Xers are the most difficult to win over, our emphasis has been on that generational group.

Let's face it. Traditionalists are dying out and Baby Boomers are retiring. An estimated 60 million are set to leave the workforce in the next 10 years. As an entrepreneur, most of your interaction will be with Xers and Millennials (who are different from Xers). Though their job performance may be lacking, however, Millennials have grandiose dreams, and are more willing than Xers to buy into a positive future of prosperity for all.

Keep in mind none of the employees represented by these generational categories are monolithic, as I personally know five or six young Millennials that are focused, committed and razor sharp. Each person will join the organization with a different skill set, intrinsic values, inadequacies, problems and contributions. Some will fit your team objectives; others will not. Be prepared to accept the inevitability of a bad hire. Develop, in advance, policies and procedures for termination. And do all you can to enable that person to find the future most compatible for them.

Leander Jackie Grogan

CHAPTER 2

Types of Organizations

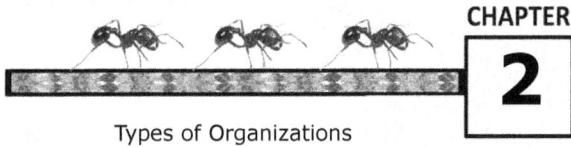

*A*lan Murray, national business analyst and deputy managing editor of The Wall Street Journal, Robin Hanson, renowned economist at George Mason University, and Forrest W. Breyfogle, III, Professional Engineer and ASQ Fellow are among the international management theorists and deep-thinkers trying to prepare us for the next great paradigm shift in the marketplace. For almost a decade, they've been singing the same profound, unsettling song:

We are poised to see the end of management as we know it. Organizations from this point forward will never be the same.

Such a weighty prediction is enough to keep CEOs up late, burning the midnight oil. With such compelling evidence to back up their claims, executives all over the world are scrambling to get prepared.

I've heard some wild predictions in my lifetime including

Y2K, the massive deaths that would be caused by killer bees migrating from South America, and the coming worldwide catastrophe of 2012. I was around when sales analyst predicted Christmas internet sales would eventually surpass brick and mortar retail sales. The stigma of credit card security has evaporated, compared to those early days of skepticism, and decrepit old Baby Boomers like me, with declining energy levels, arthritic aches and pains and personal concerns about being mugged in the parking lot, are increasingly staying inside, buying over the home computer screen rather than at the local mall.

In 2009, even with the economic downturn, online Christmas sales were up $27 billion or 6%. By 2018, if trends continue to hold, the prediction of more Christmas sales online than in physical stores will come true.

Experts correctly predicted the browning of America's workforce back in the seventies, global warming's impact on free market economies in the eighties, the explosion of Hispanic growth and sobering dependence on illegal immigration in the nineties, and the catastrophic shortfall of state and local fiscal budgets in the 2000's. What is this new prediction about the end of management and why is it so important to small business owners?

The advent of management systems in the 20th century was a much-needed innovation to control masses of workers, unstable resources, complex assembly lines, and distribution channels never seen before the industrial revolution. Managers were viewed as heroes who came in and developed systems to tame the unruly beasts known as business organizations. Visionaries like Henry Ford and John D. Rockefeller created complex metrics and automated systems to harness the maximum production of man and machine.

But with these systems came the ugly by-products of bureaucracy, political entrenchment and self-perpetuation. More and more, managers became bureaucrats making decisions based on their private agendas and instinct to survive.

It was a classic case of the dark side of human nature taking over? People routinely rejected the call to give up power in order to usher in a more qualified leader or superior plan of action? No one was willing to go quietly into the night? Only one thought prevailed and that was the ability to survive at all cost.

Infighting, Turf Wars and Self-Preservation

A composite of this survival mentality can be seen in the current gridlock between the White House and both Houses of Congress. Everyone knows the systems of healthcare, education and tax assessment are broken. But with so many vested interests and political agendas, how can enough people come together to fix the problem.

Look at it this way. If 50% of your campaign contributions came from the beer companies, what kind of selfless, high principled Ralph Nader crusader would you have to be to vote for a ban on alcohol?

I can hear you now. "Distinguished ladies and gentlemen of the House of Representatives, my humble recommendation is that we adjourn for the weekend and settle our minor differences over an ingenuously drunken delectation of Budweiser mini-kegs."

So it has become with managers, drunk on power within the corporations. Territorial wars are being waged, power struggles continue to escalate and precious human capital is being expended on issues which have nothing to do with the efficiency of the organization.

I mentioned the Hershey's Corporation's entire Board of Directors resigning. This is an excellent example of the ongoing power struggles that persist in most large organizations. To make a long story short, the Hershey's Board of Directors, along with the CEO, is responsible for running the company. But the charitable trust, the Hershey's Trust Board, has veto power over everything the corporate board does. Back in 2002, Wrigley offered to buy Hershey's for the sweet sum of $12.5 billion. The CEO and corporate board said yes, but the Trust Board turned it down. And then the Trust Board proceeded to announce publicly that it was unhappy with the corporation's earning performance.

Hey, isn't this the same corporation that garnered a $12.5 billion buyout offer with a hefty premium over the stock price, an offer you "Trust Board" people just turned down?

Another nasty fight broke out when, against the wishes of powerful board members, Hewlett-Packard acquired Compaq Computer in a $25 billion stock swap. When the dust settled, Carleton "Carly" Fiorina, the first woman chairman and chief executive of HP, was forced to resign.

There are thousands of stories of power struggles and infighting throughout corporate America. The problem is, with the hyperactive, accelerated volatility of the marketplace, these unproductive management practices have placed respective companies in jeopardy.

Globalization, deregulation, accelerated convergence, protracted litigation strategies and rapid technological innovation have combined in a perfect storm of destruction to wipe out formidable, well known, highly-praised market leaders in the blink of an eye.

Perhaps, you remember when Blockbuster Video was king of the hill. Back in 1985, using a Wal-Mart style brick and mortar business model, Blockbuster entered the video tape and DVD rental market, quickly driving many of its mom-and-pop competitors out of business. By 2004, Blockbuster was a cash cow with 9100 stores in 25 countries, and a commanding market share of 43%.

Then along came a spider and sat down beside her. Its name was Netflix which had developed a "cool" Xer-friendly process by which customers could sign up online for a monthly subscription and have the movies delivered to their door. With the population growing more time-starved and internet credit card transactions becoming more trustworthy, the marketplace opened up to a viable alternative to visiting physical locations. Years earlier, change and diversification of product deliver had been discussed within Blockbuster's strategic brain trust. But opposing views created a stalemate and nothing was done until it was too late.

The primary problem Netflix created for Blockbuster was the elimination of $250 million in late fee revenue to which the company had grown accustomed. It also put pressure on Blockbuster to create an online interface equal to or better than Netflix's user-friendly approach to delivering the same product. Blockbuster's unsavory, mistake-riddled online service turned out to be a laughingstock. Even with $3 billion in revenue in 2009, Blockbuster's outdated business model and sleazy practices were just too much to overcome.

Fast-forward to 2010:

Dearly beloved, we are gathered together today to announce the bankruptcy filing of Blockbuster Video. Those of you who spent so many years paying late fees and standing in line, waiting for a movie to come in, will have to find some other form of amusement to occupy your time.

I know what I'm going to do. I'm going over to Washington Mutual Bank, draw some money out of my account and go to Circuit City to buy me some VCR movies. The GM dealership is a few blocks away. Maybe, I'll stop by to see if the new Saturn Vue has come in, or maybe test drive a new Pontiac G8. All that shopping is sure to make me hungry, so I'll waltz into Steak & Ale to have a glass of that upscale Charles Shaw Merlot 2001 and devour one of those great salads.

You get the picture. In these turbulent times, you are here today and gone tomorrow ... no, gone today.

This may come as a shock to you, but the primary reason

for these ongoing internal confrontations and non-negotiable stale-mates is the classic battle between innovation and the status quo. There are hundreds of books on *change* management because the implementation of change in an organization can be a company's worst nightmare.

Within the bureaucracies that have built up over the years, the flash point is not about who's right and who's wrong, or what's best for the company and what's not best. Instead, it is about who will benefit and who will suffer.

If I manage the East coast units and you manage the West Coast units, and the company decides to merge all units, who will be the manager left standing? And if it's not me, how will that impact my career path and salary?

Let me rehearse my recommendations out loud:

- I don't think it's a good idea.
- It doesn't make sense for our operation.
- The timing is not right.
- It's going to cost too much.
- It's going to cause confusion and send the wrong signal.
- We need to study it a bit longer.

As an entrepreneur, it's important you recognize how change will potentially be received within your organization. There is a fear factor, followed by an effort to discourage or even sabotage the new agenda. Don't take it personally. People are just trying to survive.

Resistance to change extends far beyond the business arena. Austrian economist Joseph Schumpeter refers to a century old cultural phenomenon that perpetually opposes change, especially change based on accelerated growth. It's called *creative destruction.* It's the belief that as the creative process unfolds, rapid change always destroys the old to make way for the new. In that process, it detaches us from our roots and those values, priorities and beliefs that made us who we are.

The industrial revolution is an excellent example of this phenomenon. It unraveled our agrarian society, displaced family units, elevated corruption and greed, took mothers out of the home and into the factories, polluted the air, drove up prices and in essence, changed the world forever. But in the process, it made us the most powerful nation in the world.

That is still the most profound argument against using creative destruction as a justification to resist change. We simply cannot ignore the end results. Whether we agree with it or not, change has always been the engine that gave us the potential to soar like eagles, to be better in the future than we were in the past.

But change is a two-edged sword. It can reward as well as destroy. In fact, most effective change cannot be implemented without creating casualties. Thus, we find ourselves face to face with the original dilemma that continues to polarize large organizations. If change is implemented, who will be left standing? Who will the casualties be?

Pressured by an evolving marketplace, and desperately needing innovation in order to survive, most small businesses have no choice. They must constantly embrace change. This mindset, along with the minimal bureaucracy through which change must flow, gives small businesses a strategic advantage over large corporations. Remember, the more layers of management within an organization, the greater the chances change will be suppressed.

In his book, *The Innovator's Dilemma*, Clayton M. Christensen explains how difficult it is for innovation to reach the top. Resistance, especially in the United States, is built into the current management apparatus. And with capital in the bank, there is no need to correct bad market assumptions right away.

With small business organizations, however, innovation has a much greater chance of surviving and actually being implemented. The bureaucracy that lobbies for the status quo will not have been firmly established in your company. This gives you a competitive advantage to receive, evaluate, and implement game-changing strategies before large business can capitalize on the opportunity.

Based on what the deep-thinkers are saying, are all businesses and management systems in trouble?

The simple answer is yes, to varying degrees. I'm sure it would be difficult to envision Google, with a stock price hovering above $525 per share, being in trouble. But eighteen years ago, Blockbuster was where Google is now. The prevailing wisdom suggests all companies have points of vulnerability. We wake up in the morning and hear on the news that, not only has the Justice Department forced Google to break up, but someone has created a Google worm which has permanently destroyed all of its servers and stolen all of its proprietary secrets. Then what?

Types of Organizations

To best understand which businesses are most vulner-able, you must understand the nature of each type of organization. By understanding the organizational types, you can determine whether your small business is compatible with the marketplace and customer base it serves.

Back in 1979, management theorist Henry Mintzberg

published *The Structuring of Organizations* which identified five distinct organizational structures: simple structure, machine bureaucracy, professional bureaucracy, divisionalized form, and adhocracy. These structures differ in many ways, and are useful in the distribution of power and control throughout the organization.

Simple Structure

The simple structure is indicative of its name, facilitating a lean, entrepreneurial style organization with a few owner/manager individuals in control of primary decision-making, supervision and profit sharing. A manageable group of subordinates is delegated responsibilities designed to carry out the company's basic tasks. Employee interaction is very informal; little of its behavior is standardized or formalized, and minimal use is made of planning, training, and liaison devices.

Machine Bureaucracy

The machine bureaucracy is the offspring of the industrial revolution with emphasis on standardizing all tasks for easy coordination and the creation of low skilled, highly specialized jobs. This system requires many analysts to maintain specific systems to control behavior on lower levels. For instance, on an auto assembly line, should workers install the heater or air conditioner first? A specialist in systems analysis and design must determine the most efficient processes to deploy.

Generally, machine bureaucracies involve dull, repetitive work centered on mass production. Employees become efficient through specialization, performing a task over and over again. Without the need for creativity, adaptability or sociability, certain extroverted personality types feel isolated and deprived of the privilege to think or interact with other employees on a more consistent basis.

Professional Bureaucracy

The professional bureaucracy, unlike the machine bureaucracy, relies on the standardization of skills rather than workplace processes. Because it relies on trained professionals, that is, skilled individuals who must be given considerable control over their own work, the organization surrenders a good deal of its power not only to the professionals themselves, but also to the associations and institutions that initially train them. This is indicative of the hospital system where doctors receive standardized training and must be trusted to carry out their skills with little direct supervision.

Professional bureaucracies are best suited for organizations that find themselves in a complex environment where control is decentralized so that skilled individuals can work with autonomy.

It should come as no surprise that standardized skills tend to suppress adaptability. Facing certain unforeseen challenges, employees apply the knowledge they already possess rather than innovate new ways of doing things. In this way, the professional bureaucracy is a clear-cut deterrent to innovation.

Divisionalized Form

The divisionalized form is represented by individual divisions within an organization with a variety of product lines joined together by a loose overlay of administration. Each division is autonomous, but subject to performance controls generated by standardized metrics originating from the home office or main headquarters. A good example of this structure can be seen in the Procter & Gamble organization. There are many products with many divisions. Each division is granted a certain amount of autonomy to reach specific goals. Managers do not have people standing over their shoulder. Rather, the governing mechanisms are the goals themselves.

The divisionalized form is unique in that it is not a complete structure but a partial structure, superimposed on other structures within the divisions. It was created to resolve problems created by the machine bureaucracy inability to adapt. By overlaying another level of administration that had the flexibility to add and subtract divisions, the organization found a way to adapt itself to new conditions and spread its potential risks.

Unfortunately, just when we need to depend more on innovation and lightning fast decision-making to survive the turbulent marketplace, this administration creates a top layer of bureaucracy which discourages both risk-taking and innovation. Managers are more inclined to hit their numbers with tried and true methodologies, rather than experiment with new ways of doing things.

Adhocracy

The adhocracy is both complex and non-standardized. It relies on specialized experts to get the bulk of the work done. But in this case, the experts must work together to create new things instead of working apart to perfect established skills. With power and authority based on expertise rather than titles, the traditional manager/subordinate relationship evaporates. People become powerful within the organization based on the number of skills they've perfected.

The dynamic nature of autocracies requires employees who are both intellectual and goal-driven. Each challenge is treated as a new phenomenon deserving a fresh approach rather than a standardized solution. Experts must cooperate with each other to achieve a successful outcome. Autocracies represent the only configuration that combines some sense of democracy with an absence of bureaucracy.

In watching a film company make a movie, although the

director is in charge, he or she is involved in a constant interchange with lighting experts, videographers, actors and financiers. On any given day, the cameraman can be seen telling the director what to do. This is the essence of an autocracy. Flexibility and collaboration are the driving forces behind success.

Let's revisit the concept of polarity management where there may be more than one right answer. In this instance, your small business may be more than one organizational type.

Say you own a three-person screening business where candidates, seeking employment at other companies, are sent to you to be screened for urine, drug and blood pressure abnormalities. Your daily traffic is made up of jobseekers trying to get across the final health and legal hurdles in order to get hired. Your actual clients, however, are the companies that pay you to do the screening. It's a small-office. You're interaction with coworkers is informal and free from bureaucracy. For all practical purposes, your business is a simple structure.

But let's look a bit closer. The nurse in the back room that takes urine samples and blood pressure readings operates with a reasonable amount of autonomy. There's no one standing over her shoulder. She's a professional, relying on the standardization of skills rather than workplace processes. Sounds like a professional bureaucracy to me.

Let's take it a step further. Let's say one of your clients runs an oil patch company that cleans chemical storage tanks. The company is behind in meeting deadlines set by its clients to have a certain amount of tanks cleaned by a certain time, and the human resources manager has gone on a hiring binge. They need workers right away. But out of the last five people they've sent over, three have not passed the screening. The human resources manager calls and says, "I need you to do what you can to get these people through."

When you opened your company, you made a commitment to yourself to remain ethical, never fudge the numbers, and never get involved in shady procedures that might ultimately bring down your company. You want to help the human resources manager. But you also want to remain true to your mission.

Collaborating with the nurse you learn that two candidates have prohibitive blood pressure readings. But the readings are not that far off. She explains that in many cases, blood pressure readings accelerate because of the anxiety of being in a doctor's office, or because of the mental pressure associated with losing a job based on health reasons.

Your nurse tells you that exercise sometimes helps to bring down a patient's blood pressure. Your secretary/ administrator tells you her boyfriend is a karate black belt and heavily into Oriental nutrition. He has revealed to her that certain types of chicken soups help to bring down blood pressure. You jump on the internet and verify that Japanese researchers have done studies that show certain types of chicken soups with collagen additives do act as ACE inhibitors that helped to bring down blood pressure levels. You called the Asian food store around the corner and they have two different brands from which to choose.

You meet privately with both candidates, explaining your intent to help them pass the screening by engaging in some light exercise and eating chicken soup. They both agree to participate. You get your administrator to type up a crude permissions statement and have them sign. You go to the corner store, retrieve the soup, have the candidates eat the soup and then take turns on the treadmill. You wait a few hours, then have your nurse checked their readings again.

Both candidates pass!

Your team has not only engaged in some complex problem solving, it has actually created a new thing ... a new procedure for helping candidates get across that final employment barrier. Isn't that what movie makers do; use their specialized expertise in goal-driven, free-flowing collaboration to create a new thing. Sounds like an adhocracy to me.

One additional observation you should make about your new simple structure ... professional bureaucracy ... adhocracy organization. You have a monumental strategic advantage over larger competitors in your industry. You were able to turn on a dime, receiving the information, processing the options and implementing the solution in a matter of hours. How long would it have taken a large organization to set a meeting just to discuss the matter or get the lawyers to send over a release contract for the candidates to sign? When you think about it, you begin to realize why the old era of bureaucratic management is dying.

Resistance to Change

This is not to say all smaller organizations are open to innovation and change. I have a friend who briefly worked for a small accounting office, owned by a command-style Traditionalist and populated by yes-men Baby Boomers. The office used a non-intuitive, problematic version of Peachtree as the accounting software, WordPerfect as the document processor and some kind of email program that did not allow attachments of any kind. My friend proposed changes in the software as well some of the redundant procedures they used internally. The owner and managers were opposed to all changes.

The owner explained that, after twenty plus years in business, when he looked at his bank account he didn't see anything wrong. Why fix what wasn't broken?

In earlier discussions we mention that high levels of equity or money in the bank were deterrents to innovation in large organizations because it postponed the need for managers to ask the hard questions or correct bad market assumptions. The same holds true for smaller companies with a substantial financial cushion. If they're making money, then how could anything be wrong?

In 2008, Bear Stearns Companies, a global investment bank and securities broker reported $17 billion in previous year earnings, had $28 billion in assets on the books, and had seen a 52-week high stock price of $132. Before the year was over, the subprime derivative-infested company was sold off at fire-sale prices to JP Morgan Chase for $10 per share. In a volatile marketplace where destructive winds of change can swoop in on an organization with little or no warning, money in the bank means nothing at all.

Even when managers see red ink on the books, they often find reasons to resist change.

Many years ago, as a marketing consultant, I made a critical presentation to a midsize grocery chain. The chain had begun losing double-digit market share annually and didn't have a clue how to get their customers back.

I did the preliminary research.

Some of the older stores were in "senior citizen" neighborhoods and catered to people on fixed incomes. Some stores had 20% empty shelves and an 8% ratio of goods with expired dates. Some stores had been built with the meat department close to the front door so when you walked in, the first thing you smelled was raw fish. Some stores had tattered holes in the floor tiling, blocked only by small construction signs that read: *Beware, Use Caution,* etc. Some stores had no lighting in the parking lot. Although these few stores closed at 6 p.m., at 6 p.m. in the winter, it was already dark outside.

Here's a big one. Most of their competitors had slowly migrated to UPC bar coding at the checkout counter. This chain still had cashiers looking at each product and pecking in the price on the cash register's iron keys.

A father and two sons ran the total operation. When I started my presentation, the youngest son and a district manager sat in the conference room, quietly listening. About ten minutes into the presentation, the younger son got up to go get his older brother. About twenty minutes into the presentation, the older brother got up to go get his father.

With all the organization's decision-makers present, the conference room felt like a mausoleum, somber faces staring at the screen. I stood there, telling them much of what they already knew, but were afraid to address.

I saved the worst news for last. I told them even if they fixed all of the structural and cosmetic problems that I had identified, their brand had lost so much appeal, they could never expect to bring all of the previous customers back.

What they desperately needed was a comprehensive rebranding, not necessarily a name change, but a reinvigorated image which appealed to a slightly different customer. I explained the climbing divorce rate, the propensity of mothers having children out of wedlock and changing the composition and definition of the American family, the growing emphasis on health consciousness, the inability of their large chunk of fixed-income senior citizen customers to respond to volume promotions, and our need to make the trip to the store a total shopping experience based on the emergence of a new, younger, less traditional shopper.

The father was visibly angry. He had spent his whole life building the chain from scratch, only to have a young college boy, armed with research and metrics and fancy strategies come in and tell him in the presence of his sons that his stores were a failure.

It was when I told him about the "lifestyle experience"

strategy I had in mind that tensions reached a boiling point.

I proposed revamping stores with bright colors and electronic screens and hourly giveaways announced over the Intercom system. I wanted goofy mechanical heads, smacking candy mouths and reciting original "sweet-tooth" nursery rhymes on the candy aisle and juggling clowns outside and a donkey ride for the kids. I wanted shopping carts that made the sound of race cars and recordings of chickens cackling in the egg department. I wanted food experts coming in, setting up display tables, talking about new recipes and giving stuff away. I wanted a "singles" board (there was no eHarmony) in the front of the store where groups could announce parties and make connections. I wanted a holiday raffle on the laughable, gimpy-looking new Japanese Toyota Corollas that had started to be imported into the country.

He said to me: Do you really think I'm going to sit here and let you turn my store into a circus?

He got up and told his older son to cut me a check for my time and send me on my way.

Fast forward ten years later. All but two of the stores had been closed. The remaining two locations had been turned into neighborhood emporiums with a small but loyal customer following.

Sometimes change is too painful to implement. Your team may eventually come to you and recommend you dismantle the very product line with which you started the business. I wonder how the old managers at Polaroid felt when they discontinued the instant film cameras? Millennials are sitting there, reading this book and wondering, "What is this thing called instant film?"

By the way, I've got an old SyQuest Removable Drive and an IBM Selectric II in my garage if anyone is interested in making an offer. You never know when your computer is going to go on the blink.

As we move into Chapter Three, you should be loaded for bear. Now that you have an historical perspective of management and the stagnating, self-perpetuating practices that threaten its existence, it's time to take a closer look at your small business and how it will evolve with you at the helm, trying to create a *new thing*.

Tighten your seat belt. The bumpiest road is just ahead.

CHAPTER

3

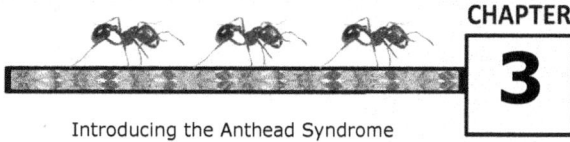

Introducing the Anthead Syndrome

*W*hat will the new small business model look like? In a word: *chaotic*. It will resemble a colony of skillful, aggressive, meticulously trained ants, loosely directed by a queen and a few drones, scouring the countryside for opportunities that benefit the entire mound.

The more scientists study ants (Formicidae), the more amazed they are by the sophisticated socialization, delegation of power and efficiency in task completion. To observe a million ants, operating as one unified superorganism, assuming multiple roles at critical interval and demonstrating an invisible synergy unmatched by any other species is truly a thing of beauty.

Some species like the trap-jaw ants from Costa Rica can accelerate at 100,000 times the force of gravity with speeds up to 145 mph. Other smaller, more docile ants like the Allomerus workers in Africa specialize in stealth-like attacks on insects five to ten times their size. Each colony consists of castes of labor special-ists that assume responsibility for a designated portion of the work. However, at any given instance, a scout, responsible for finding food, might turn into a worker, responsible for hauling the food back to the mound, might turn into a soldier, responsible for defending the colony against invaders. A single ant goes from predator to transporter to protector.

I call it the "Anthead Syndrome®."

Envision your employees pulling into the parking lot each morning. As they step out of their vehicles, they put on a mask that resembles an ant's head. When they enter the building, you are unable to distinguish one employee from another, except by the tasks they perform. The tasks would be determined by the urgency of need based on metrics and other predetermined indicators that notified each worker of that day's priorities.

It might sound a bit Orwellian, but as a young contract web designer in Austin, Texas, I had the opportunity to experience it, firsthand.

Arriving at work one morning, I was asked to go into the conference room with the rest of the staff. The owner came in to explain his concerns. After looking at the sales projections for the month, the company had fallen critically behind. He wanted us to abandon all normal activities or assignments, get on the phone and call at least fifty people. It didn't matter to him how we develop our lists, whether it be Yellow Pages, church membership lists, voter registration lists, small businesses, personal friends or teachers and administrators. The objective was to contact at least fifty people to tell them about our web development company and let them know a commitment from anyone they referred within the next twenty-four hours would be worth a substantial discount to the client and referral fee to them.

By the next afternoon, the phones were ringing off the hook. Although the customer conversion rate was less than 10%, the effort generated enough revenue to get the company's sales back on track. Within forty-eight hours, everyone was able to resume working in their designated areas of specialization.

Personally, I didn't like the idea of having to sell. I begrudgingly called my fifty people, but felt quite awkward in the process. At the end of the month, when he handed out restaurant gift cards to reward us for our spontaneous cooperation, I felt quite guilty. I wanted to give the card back, but the thought of those grilled shrimp overpowered my budding sense of workplace integrity.

The Anthead Syndrome® is predicated upon a complex process called *polymorphism* which means having multiple forms. In the context of your small business, you will be hiring employees, not based on a specific task, but rather a specific range of skills. Their contribution to the organization will "morph" based on the needs generated in that particular time frame.

Though no longer considered a small business with its $10 billion in worldwide sales, multi-level marketer Avon serves as an excellent example of the Anthead Syndrome. Although Avon representatives have the primary duty of selling, they are also responsible for recruiting, mentoring and training others to succeed within the network. On any given day, you might find a top sales representative doing absolutely no sales at all. Rather, she is engaged in network-building or specialty training of new recruits.

It's no secret that we are better at performing some tasks, than others. Some ant species survive because of their superior ability to find food; others, because they can defend and protect the storage facilities where the food is being kept.

Sales types are better at finding the business while accounting types are better at keeping the money in the bank. The Anthead Syndrome® system, which we will refer to as "Anthead System" for short, takes this into consideration in its design of the hiring process.

Core Competencies

In her article, *Five Personal Core Competencies of the 21st Century*, Professor Helen Haste of Harvard Graduate School of Education identifies certain strengths and weakness in potential hires that help us to overcome existing deficiencies in our own organization. Under the Anthead System, we are not only hiring workers to cover an anticipated range of activities, we are hiring them to compensate for our own weaknesses as entrepreneurs.

One of the most crucial mistakes small business owners make is hiring people that looked, act and think just like them. It's a natural instinct to consider our personal attributes the best combination for success. We see ourselves as being fair, innovative, aggressive and ethical. And although this might be true, these attributes surface in varying shades and degrees which may or may not sync to the challenge at hand. When people say *no*, I take them at their word. But a good salesperson doesn't hear *no*. If I hire salespeople just like me, nothing is going to get sold.

It's important we understand what core competencies really are. Core competencies represent an individual's fundamental knowledge, ability, and/or expertise in a specific skill set. Core implies the individual has an intrinsic inclination toward matters in a specific area and is an ideal candidate for future learning in that area and related areas.

A good example would be Millennials and their core familiarity with digital, internet-related products. Conversely, give a Traditionalist an Android phone and he needs a couple of days to figure out how to turn it on.

Core competencies are determined by analyzing a combination of skills and personality traits. I know a mobile mechanic that can tear down a motor and put it back together again blindfolded. But he never shows up when he says he's going to and his price always goes up, slightly. Because I know about his background, I'm confident he's not trying to bait and switch with a higher cost. He'll quote an excellent price on rebuilding your transmission. But he'll forget to tell you that when the thing is back in your car, someone's going to have to buy five cans of transmission fluid. The problem lies in his inability to manage time and perceived auxiliary costs.

If you considered hiring him, you couldn't afford to look at his technical abilities, exclusively. You'd have to evaluate his personality traits and whether they could be altered through training. Perhaps, your operational procedures would totally eliminate his need to get involved with pricing, and a punch-in time clock would take care of the tardiness.

In your small business, each hire will be a balance between skills and personality traits. We'll talk more about this in future chapters. But for now, just know it will be virtually impossible to find a candidate that scores 100% in both areas of measurement.

According to Harvard Professor, Helen Haste, there are five critical core competencies we should carefully evaluate:

The Ability to Manage Ambiguity

Ambiguity is that fuzzy gray area between black and white, characterized by uncertainty and lack of order and/or structure, often leading to chaos and failure. It is counterintuitive to our search for linear solutions, and quite often, pushes us into the area of polarity management. We've already discussed the extent to which most managers are uncomfortable abandoning their tried-and-true, preconceived solutions in favor of unorthodox forays into the unknown. After all, how do you manage the unknown? How much of the company's money should be devoted to "string theory"? I can't see them. I don't know what the little devils do. Yet, some grumpy old Caltech scientist with an over-sized head is asking me to invest millions in a research project with no visible return in sight.

How do you think the managers at NASA felt trying to get to the moon, or CNN executives felt leaving correspondents inside of Iraq in 2003 as the bombs fell all around them? There was no playbook to follow, no way to fully measure the impact of each precarious decision.

From a parallel business perspective, how would you manage the unknown in terms of both the creative and implementation stages? If you worked for Levi Strauss in 1986, how would you respond to some young dreadlock fashion designer who came in and told you to invest your entire budget into pre-faded, stone-washed ripped-up jeans?

"Let me get this straight. We're going to take a perfectly good pair of designer jeans, spot-fade the color like zebra stains and then cut nasty little jagged slits into the legs so tattered strings hang out. Then, we're going to sell them as brand new jeans for twice the normal price? Is that what you're telling me?"

As a small business owner, there will be times when innovation reaches your desk wrapped in a troublesome package of ambiguity. You can't fully measure all of the potential outcomes. In fact, you can't even identify the process that will lead to these outcomes. How do you manage these unknowns?

The answer is not simple. But basically you manage the known's surrounding the unknowns.

So I can't know whether the jeans will sell. But I can look at the research that suggests they have the potential to sell. And if the research is not compelling, then I can look at the person who presented the idea. That person has a "known" track record. Like the bookies in Las Vegas, I can place some statistical odds on his or her potential for success.

What if a Hollywood director came to you and said, "I'm giving you first dibs on a film, the likes of which has never been made before. I'm pretty sure I'm going to run over budget, but since I'm using a new type of technology, I can't say exactly how much, nor can I say exactly when the film will be complete. And, you're going to have to pay me $350 million to direct it. Are you interested or not?"

If you're familiar with the business, your first inclination will be to tell the director to take a hike. Most anyone can hire an A-list Hollywood director with tons of credits for $5 - $20 million a picture. Three hundred and fifty million is ridiculous ... Unless you're able to look into the future to understand that this is James Francis Cameron offering you *Avatar,* the top-selling movie of all times, which will gross $2.7 billion worldwide.

You don't know what this new thing will do. What you do know is this is the same director who made *The Terminator, Aliens, and the Titanic.* He's the same guy who co-developed the digital 3-D Fusion Camera System and offered to give back his own money to Fox Studios during production to keep them from panicking about his budget overruns.

The ambiguities surrounding the project are huge. But you can manage them by determining the probability that, in the end, Cameron will deliver. If, in your evaluation, the probability is high enough, you will most likely take the deal. This is the kind of progressive thinking you want from your team and potential hires. In fact, in the interviewing process, as you probe competing candidates, this is one of the primary attributes you hope to uncover.

The Ability to Assume Agency and Responsibility

How well does a team member claim ownership of a challenge and understand the true ramifications of its success or failure? Being an effective agent means being able to maneuver through, around and over multiple obstacles with the confidence he or she can actually make a difference.

Assuming agency is similar to becoming the spokesperson for an issue or movement. The underlying premise is based on an individual's perception the issue is worth the potential risks and/or rewards associated with the project.

Former Vice President Al Gore won a Nobel Prize by taking personal responsibility for the plight of global warming and its overall impact on the environment. Public advocate Ralph Nader led a legendary one-man campaign against the *Unsafe At Any Speed* Chevrolet Corvair. Enron Vice President and whistle-blowers Sherron S. Watkins was selected as one of three "People of the Year 2002" by *Time Magazine* for her unrelenting effort to expose the illegal accounting schemes at Enron.

Whether the organization is large or small, taking public ownership of an issue or moment can come with a price. As we mentioned earlier, Carleton "Carly" Fiorina was forced out of Hewlett-Packard for here advocacy of the Compaq merger. And how can we forget the horrible persecution of Jeffrey Wigand, the Brown & Williamson maverick executive who exposed the capacity of cigarettes to addict and kill us?

The point is this. By showing a willingness to take owner-ship, team members are also demonstrating a certain leadership quality that every small business needs: The willingness to be a risk taker. After all, isn't that what you are? Isn't that what your business is all about? And aren't these the type of people you want to help your business grow?

Finding and Sustaining Community

Managing community is about successfully connecting and interacting with others and reaching out beyond our own private worlds.

One of the reasons Facebook is so popular is its ability to facilitate our need to reach out beyond our private worlds in a positive, almost risk-free manner. We are social animals by nature. And, as much as we try to hold on to our independence, our success or failure is invariably dependent upon our interactions with others.

In *New York Times* columnist David Brooks' bestseller, *The Social Animal,* he conveys new psychological research which illustrates our deep dependency on social or personal connections. Brooks says, (contrary to what we believe) "Instead of relying on rational decisions, people tend to be influenced by their underlying, unconscious emotional state, which is in turn influenced by the social relationships surrounding them."

Fear is a great deterrent to our ability to effectively reach out to others. Sometimes, it's the fear of rejection or reprisal. Other times, our reluctance is based on our fear of non-recognition and a selfish desire to avoid sharing the limelight.

Under the Anthead System, the importance of sociability will increase tenfold, as the system, itself, emphasizes the team concept to the maximum degree. Managing community will be critical in all facets of your operation and indispensable in your effort to achieve stated organizational goals.

Managing Emotion

It means the entire team should understand emotion and

reason (logic) are both connected. Decisions based on these opposing drivers may override each other, but will seldom be totally separate from each other.

"I don't like Suzanne." This statement reflects a counter-productive attitude and has the potential to kill an entire project.

It shouldn't be that way. People should be able to separate their personal feelings from the work at hand. But we know better. Yet, some managers try to force logic into the equation by threatening both parties to either work together or hit the road.

Successfully managing emotions begins with recognizing the huge impact they have on our day-to-day lives. The objective is not to eliminate emotions from the workplace, but to separate the good from the bad, and then weed out the bad.

Imagine the CEO crying at a Christmas party when the announcement is made the company was able to feed fifty needy families in the community. Would you want to eliminate that scene simply because it's emotionally driven?

Now think about two team members who refused to speak to each over a long-standing dispute. Would you want that kind of emotionally-driven behavior to continue? Somewhere along the line anger, frustration and/or resentment have arisen. You can't just bully the offended parties into pretending it never happened.

Managing emotions in this situation may involve bringing the combatants together in a face-to-face sit-down with a third party mediator, or forcing the parties to submit in writing their perception of the root cause of the dispute, which, by the way may be complicated and multi-layered and interrupted differently by each party. The main thing is to sit down with the parties to make them aware of the long-term consequences of their collective behavior. Then, move toward repairing the riff, fully aware the triggers you discover may not be the least bit logical or worthy of the dissension they've caused.

Managing Technological Change

Technological tools help us to do things more efficiently. The same tools are also capable of gradually changing our core social practices, similar to the way Facebook and Twitter have impacted the preferred methods of communication in today's society. Sometimes, instead of us managing the tools, the tools end up managing us (online poker addiction).

From a hiring perspective, we want individuals that will "fit" in our organization, regardless of their specific roles. Realizing, under the Anthead System, these roles may change from day to day, this "fit" proposition becomes very important. You're seeking people who can interact with all types, regardless of their background or area of expertise, and learn the technology as they go.

Baby Boomers often struggle to keep up with the new technology and that's okay. All you're really asking for is a willingness to learn and adapt. Their true value is measured in their strategic savvy gained over time; knowledge that Xers have not yet accumulated. Their designation as a "fit" has little to do with the technology.

When I was a teenager, working during the summer to buy my first car, I landed a job at a chemical refinery in Pasadena, Texas. My second day there, I witnessed an argument between the head carpenter and the head pipefitter. They both wanted Pedro in their crew for that day.

Pedro was a Hispanic laborer who worked for the pipefitters, carpenters, and sheet metal workers. He was the only laborer that worked for all three groups. Everyone liked him. He knew exactly which tools and supplies were needed for each job. He spoke English and Spanish which allowed him to interpret the crew leader's instructions to other laborers. He endured the racial jokes and lunch hour pranks with a smile. And although we were working a sixty-day shutdown (seven days per week, 12 hours per day) he never seemed to get weary or short tempered. He was somewhat of a celebrity in his own right.

Then, one day he didn't come in. We found out later he had been arrested for driving while intoxicated. It wasn't his first time.

My takeaway was being a perfect worker and pleasing everyone came at a very high psychological price. As a small business owner, if you're looking to hire a perfect worker, I suggest you keep a lot of Jack Daniels around. Both, you and the worker are going to need it.

Here's a cold, hard fact. In today's complex society, current hiring predicators such as stress interviews, psychological tests and surveys, role-playing, situational platforming and focus group analysis are woefully inadequate in uncovering the whole person. There are issues of neuroticism that seldom come to the surface until it's too late.

"Going Postal" was a slang term derived from a series of incidents starting in 1983 when angry United States Postal Service workers shot and killed managers, coworkers, and members of the general public in retaliatory acts of rage. In 2009, a father, apparently distraught over being fired from a Los Angeles medical facility, shot and killed his wife, five young children and then committed suicide at their home.

In 2011, a Cupertino, California man named Shareef Allman shot and killed three coworkers before being killed by police. The shop steward had confronted him about having multiple accidents and snagging overhead wires when Allman had inadvertently left the truck bed in the air at the quarry. Allman told others he felt the company was after him because he was African American.

And who can forget Steven Slater, the Jet Blue flight attendant who cursed out a passenger, grabbed some beers, and then slid down the plane's escape ramp after it had landed. Declining civility in society in general and management bullying, specifically, have created some tense moments in the American boiler cooker we call the workplace. There was a time when an owner could stand up, stick his chest out and tell an unproductive employee, "You're fired! You're nothing but a low-life! Get off my property!"

Now, I say to you ... be very, very afraid.

In this new system, you'll be hiring employees that don't work out. As stated in the previous chapter, do everything you can to empower them to find a situation more compatible to their skill set. Release them with empathy and try not to give them a reason to retaliate. We live in a crazy world. Govern yourself accordingly.

The Anthead Syndrome®

The Anthead Syndrome® recognizes six types of workers, critical to the success of the organization. If you decide to implement the system in your small business, you're eventually going to need them all. They are:

King/Queen
Drone/Enforcer
Scout
Worker (technical and nontechnical)
Soldier
Larvae Sacrifice

King/Queen

In every ant colony there is a queen, an overseer of sorts who has a comprehensive knowledge of the mound's humble beginnings, survival practices and proximity to other mounds. Since most small businesses are still run by men (that's quickly changing), and since most men don't care to be referred to as queens (that's quickly changing too), the small business owner in the Anthead System is known as the king/queen.

The king/queen is generally the entrepreneur who possessed the vision to start the company and knows its position in the overall marketplace. That's probably you. And if you haven't already figured it out, meeting the enormous requirements of this position is enough to start you on early heart medicine and fill your head with premature gray.

The king/queen should possess all of the basic characteristics of good leadership: exemplary character, integrity and trustworthiness, enthusiasm about the company and a passion for its mission, confidence in himself/herself and the potential of the organization, tolerance of ambiguity and composure under pressure, a commitment to excellence but tolerant of imperfection, proactive in matters of urgency, spontaneous in risk-taking and fully prepared to admit failures.

The king/queen is responsible for six critical functions:

- recruiting
- goal-setting
- inspiring
- empowering
- mentoring
- problem-solving

You probably already understand why recruiting is an indispensable component that demands your continued hands-on involvement. The Anthead System is based on polymorphism ... employees with a specific range of skills, "morphing" to the tasks at hand. They must also be able to successfully collaborate with different employee types. Not every individual is capable of operating under this system, nor do they prefer to. Remember me on the contract assignment in Austin, Texas. I had a begrudging attitude and didn't give my very best to the temporary assignment.

During the hiring process, it is very important that a candidate understand what he or she is getting into. It is equally important for the hiring manager to know precisely the skill set and character attributes for which he or she is looking. Until you are able to train someone to understand the big picture and see what you see, you must continue to "own" the recruiting and hiring function.

Goal-setting, though initially your exclusive responsibility will quickly become a collaborative effort between you and other team leaders. Notice I didn't say you and other managers. When the Anthead System is clicking on all cylinders, goal-setting becomes a collaborative effort that dips all the way down, or should I say across, the full spectrum of the organization. You'll be astounded by the useful ideas the delivery driver has. He's visited your customer's locations many more times than you, and observed patterns and tendencies you'll never see.

Inspiring others is one of the things that visionaries do best. They take an unfamiliar, untested concept and transform it into something believable, attainable, and beneficial to the participants. In a way they are legendary conmen, peddling the truth instead of a lie. They believe, then make it possible for others to believe; enduring skepticism, criticism and even sabotage along the way.

Your ability to inspire is a critical leadership characteristic and key component in the potential success of your business. It's not enough to believe, you must make others believe as well. That entails a whole range of communications skills based on research, analysis and preparation.

How can you inspire me to believe a car can actually run on vegetable oil when you know nothing about combustible engines? And what will you say when I tell you the fossil fuels used to grow the plants to make vegetable oil actually increases the pollution in the atmosphere by 35%?

Inspiring others is no pie in the sky. It's actually hard work. Even the conmen will tell you to do your research first, and then open your mouth. To inspire, you must gain trust through words and deeds. And you must be knowledgeable enough to present believable end results.

Empowering others puts forth the assumption you have power and are in a position to relinquish it or use it to give others the knowledge, tools, and support to carry out their assignments. By owning the company, you do have some power. But it's not necessarily the most effective kind of power.

Machiavellianism, named after Niccolo Machiavelli, the 16th-century Italian philosopher who wrote *The Prince*, is a term social psychologists use to describe a person's tendency to deceive and manipulate other people for their personal gain. Their approach to gaining power is "by all means necessary", which may include lying, cheating, bullying, sabotaging, and even withdrawing from the process. Back in the 60's, Richard Christie and Florence L. Geis developed the MACH-IV personality test to help hiring managers identify individuals with these unwanted tendencies.

For all practical purposes, a Machiavellian owner represents a worst case scenario. Inside the bureaucratic hierarchy of large corporations, there are some checks and balances that prevent a high MACH personality from completely devastating coworkers. But as a small business owner, high MACHs represent the ultimate source of checks and balances within the organization, with free reign to devastate the lives of employees as they see fit. In most instances, the high rate of turnover leaves the owner surrounded by yes-men with limited career options and a willingness to accept the abuse. These reward-oriented workers would never question his conduct or rebel in any way.

Machiavellian owners have power. But this is definitely not the kind of power you want. According to Steven L. McShane and Mary Ann Von Glinow, authors of *Organizational Behavior, a groundbreaking management analysis*, there are five kinds of power:

- Legitimate
- Reward
- Coercive
- Expert
- Referent

Legitimate power ... has to do with the assumption people in certain roles with certain titles can request certain behaviors of others and expect them to abide by this authority. "I'm a cop. Let me see your license."

Reward power ... refers to the ability to control the allocation of rewards valued by others. "You make your quota and I'll reward you with a bonus."

Coercive power ... refers to the ability to apply punishment and exert peer pressure. "All the other team members gave blood during the annual drive. I would hate for the boss to find out you're the only one who slacked."

Expert power ... has to do with an individual's capacity to influence others by possessing knowledge or skills that they value. "If you say we need five camera angles, Mr. Spielberg, then five angles it'll be."

Referent power ... is the most important, at least for the small business owner. Referent power is the ability to influence others because they identify with, respect and trust you. Reverent power attempts to motivate and inspire rather than control. This inspiration is most effective when owners take the time to know their employees, that is to say, their personal preferences, goals and aspirations. Owners can then align these aspirations to company priorities and show employees how their contribution can be a mutual benefit to both them and the organization as a whole. "Joan, I know you have relatives in Florida. So I'm sending you to the convention in Tampa to represent our company."

Retired CEO Jack Welch of GE, is considered by many business leaders as the last great innovator in corporate America. Back in the 1980's when GE was floundering under tons of bureaucracy and a lock on the status quo, Welch transformed the company into a world class market leader with a unique learning culture and the contemporary concept of a *boundaryless* organization. With a philosophy that managing less is managing better, he set a clear, ambitious vision and inspired other people to act.

Small business owners can learn so much from Jack Welch, primarily because he operated GE as though it were a small business, nimble, innovative and responsive to the needs of the marketplace and his team. Rather than depend on coercion and control, we should look to Welch's legendary practices utilizing reverent power as our mandate for success. Machiavellian tactics are a losing proposition in this new world economy. We must adjust our approach so the results for both owner and employee are a mutual win-win.

<u>Mentoring</u> is a key component, critical to any organization's future growth. When talking about his years at GE, Jack Welch said, "My main job was developing talent. I was a gardener providing water and other nourishment to our top 750 people. Of course, I had to pull out some weeds, too."

Mentoring is the process of sharing wisdom and proving guidance, direction, and learned techniques to other team members.

Quite often, in a hectic, time-starved environment, small business owners relegate mentoring to a lower status, thinking it's more a charitable act, designed to help individuals with their personal careers. Mentoring, however, is of mutual benefit to both the mentee and the organization. Successful companies such as Southwest Airlines and Microsoft, with high profile mentoring networks, have documented some of the tangible benefits derived from mentoring. These include the effective development of future leaders, retention of key performers and dissemination of collective knowledge critical to the organization's growth.

As an upstart, unseasoned entrepreneur, you will also find that being mentored by an experienced business veteran you respect and trust will offer a tremendous tool in assisting with future decision-making, especially if that person has a proven track record and is direct familiarity with your specific industry.

How would you like to sit down with billionaire business guru, Warren Buffett, for a one-on-one mentoring lunch? In 2008, Zhao Danyang, a money manager for the Hong Kong, paid $2.1 million. In 2010, the same privilege costs $2.6 million.

Mentoring will always be a valuable process within your organization and a responsibility that you may share, but never give up. The potential dividends are huge and provide the lubricant for your Anthead System to run efficiently and cohesively as it propels your organization into the future.

Problem-solving is another function of the king/queen that will never go away. There will always be problems, some, of which can only be solved by you.

President Harry S. Truman had a sign on his desk in the Oval office that read: *The Buck Stops Here.* It was the counter to an expression that implied people within large organizations like to "pass the buck", or shuffle the responsibility to someone else. There will be times when the final call to punt or go for it will be left totally up to you. Those are the times when problem-solving techniques will be most critical.

In the Anthead System, problems that reach the king/queen level are generally attached to an ambiguity that cannot be addressed by the collective knowledge within the organization. It's usually a new dilemma, or an old dilemma being distorted by a new set of factors.

You might have a system in place where you ship products to customers by mail. Perhaps, a customer requests a product overnight and Federal Express is the only company that delivers to that location overnight. The problem is you haven't paid the FedEx bill. They've cut off your service. Your business plan and P&L budget say one thing. Your bank account says something else. Now what?

The time frame and limited options have placed the problem squarely on your desk. You want to pay FedEx, but your largest customer hasn't paid you in two months. Even if you send FedEx a check, it won't arrive in time to remove the red flag on your account. Someone has to decide how to frame the problem and reach an acceptable solution. That someone is you.

Paying the cash rate drives the delivery cost up and basically eliminates your profit margin on that particular sale. If you call the customer and say you're unable to accommodate his or her request, it might call question to your capability to deliver customer-driven service in the future. If you tell the customer they have to pay the extra, they might cancel the order.

This one order is a minor problem in the total scheme of things. But it is indicative of the dilemmas small business owners face each day. You might decide to take the hit this one time and eat the delivery cost, or called a friend that has an account and give her cash to send your order. The point is problem-solving at the king/queen level is usually complex and never ending.

I was once told through a reliable channel that a certain board member needed a bribe in order for my consulting company to get the contract. He didn't need the money up front; only reassurance it would be forthcoming once the work began.

No one below me could make that decision. The question had to be framed in a complex legal, moral and profit context. The possibilities kept me up all night. In the end, fear, not ethics, made the decision for me. The reward, however alluring, was just not worth me going to jail.

I look at Wall Street wealth manager, Bernie Madoff, and wonder how many nights he lost sleep. There is a problem-solving technique called *contiguous association* where you search for cause and effect relationships based on the proximity of words or phrases. For instance, if he wrote down "must protect the status quo", the words in proximity might be "lie to people everyday"; or if he wrote "stop the years of fraud and come clean", proximity might be "too late for forgiveness, end only through prison or death."

The decision to drop the atomic bomb on Japan involved hundreds of people: the spies that kept track of Germany's effort to build a bomb, the scientist that built America's bomb, the military personnel that tested the bomb, the advisor's that advocated or opposed the bomb. But in the end, the final decision had to be made by President Harry S. Truman. Like it or not, the buck stopped with him.

As the king/queen of your organization, there will be many time the buck will stop with you. Don't be afraid to take on the challenge and make your best decision. Problem-solving will always be an imperfect science. Learn from your mistakes. As Jack Welch once said, "I've learned that mistakes can often be as good a teacher as success."

Take your lumps and move on.

Drone/Enforcer

If you're a Star Trek fan and followed the series featuring Captain Kathryn Janeway of the USS Voyager, fighting the Borg, you'll remember her first officer, Commander Chakotay. Chakotay represented the ideal depiction of what a drone/enforcer should be.

In nature, the drone ant has the primary function of mating with the queen. What a delightful job description. From a broader perspective, however, a drone has the responsibility of carrying on or carrying out the perpetuation of the species. The drone closely resembles the queen and generally stays in close proximity with her, at least temporarily, until he flies off and dies.

Under the Anthead System, the drone/enforcer doesn't fly off and die. He stays close to the small business owner, carrying on or carrying out the perpetuation of the organization.

Xers and Millennials are probably not old enough to remember. But if you had the opportunity to read about the civil rights movement, you observed Reverend Ralph David Abernathy always by the side of Reverend Martin Luther King, Jr. He was the drone/enforcer within the organization, just as Vice President Dick Cheney was within the Bush administration.

The drone/enforcer is a designated, trustworthy, hand-picked team leader that thoroughly understands the stated and unstated mission of the organization, and functions as a trumpeter of the core message, a process-server of the detailed execution of policies derived from the core message, and a transparent firewall between the owner's visionary leadership activities and responsibilities for the daily operation.

Though fiercely loyal, he is by no means a yes-man. He's not afraid to question, challenge, correct and even express disappointment in the small business owner's decision-making. But because of his respect and loyalty, these critical exchanges almost always occur behind the scenes.

As an enforcer, it is his primary responsibility to make sure the ambitious vision of the owner is carried out in both word and deed. He's neither rude nor overbearing; but rather, firm and demanding. In a real world scenario, most employees would rather be called in to the owner's office, than into his.

There is a sophisticated premise in play here that you should understand. In law enforcement, they refer to it as the "good cop/bad cop" syndrome. The criminal tends to respond based on his perception the good cop is more reasonable and has the accused individual's best interest at heart. In the business arena, and specifically in your organization, the objective is to isolate the owner (as much as possible) from being the bad cop and making sure his visionary image is not associated with unpleasant news.

"Attention! All shore leave has been canceled. We are shipping out tonight into shark infested waters off the coast of North Korea to prepare for a bloody invasion."

Whom do you suspect would make that announcement to the soldiers? Not the Admiral who planned the war. Not the ship's Captain who will be transporting the soldiers into battle. Rather, it will be the drone/enforcer, a lower ranking officer accustomed to dealing directly with the assault group, one-on-one.

When the owner wants to fire salesperson Bennie for cursing out a key customer, it is the drone/enforcer that steps in and says, "Bennie's son just got killed in a motorcycle accident last weekend. The guy is not himself right now. Let's give him another chance."

Dick Cheney knew a lot more about the details of the operation and the operatives or functionaries inside the administration than did George Bush. This superior knowledge serves as a balancing mechanism that defuses potential ego clashes when the owner is standing at the podium, smiling, waving, and having his photo taken as he receives the Entrepreneur of the Year Award. The drone/enforcer is content, knowing true power lies in superior knowledge rather than the pomp and circumstance of bright lights and formal ceremonies.

If you haven't already noticed, in most systems there is a search for balance, a point of interaction where all parties feel important, empowered and impactive in their particular roles. Because of the shifting workload and ambiguity of titles, the Anthead System is especially demanding of balance between team members. When executed correctly, participants vacillate between loosely defined roles of leadership and follow-ship, based on experience, skills and authorship of the best solution.

Under the Anthead System, balance is more an ingrained attitude than a management hierarchy. The official organizational chart is good to have as a rough starting point. But true balance is achieved when team members are willing to take on and give up responsibility based on their experience and skill set.

With which would you rather do battle, a great white shark or a black wilderness bear? The obvious answer is: depending on where the battle is waged, land or sea. As a brave warrior, I'll tangle with a great white on the Yellowstone National Park picnic grounds, a day or so after he's beached himself and had a chance to settle in.

Different challenges require different skill sets. It's counterproductive for the owner to demand that she handle an issue just because she's the boss. You don't want to see

Captain Janeway down in the engine room tampering with the warp drive. There are people better suited for that. In many instances the drone/enforcer is better suited to take on a complex challenge, even though you are the boss.

As the owner, the ultimate source of instruction, policy, and methodology, one of your key responsibilities will be mentoring the drone/enforcer. The same positive character attributes for which you chose him ... loyalty, firmness, and a stickler for detail ... can quickly turn into dictatorial rudeness, vindictiveness and a preoccupation with controlling others through coercion and fear.

English historian, Sir John Dalberg-Acton once said: *"Power tends to corrupt, and absolute power corrupts absolutely. Great men are almost always bad men, even when they exercise influence and not authority: still more when you superadd the tendency or certainty of corruption by full authority. There is no worse heresy than the fact that the office sanctifies the holder of it."*

Roughly interrupted, it means few men or women can resist the lure of power, especially absolute power. And, if the owner turns her head and allows the drone/enforcer to go unchecked, he will eventually succumb to the lure.

Note. In an organization, regardless of its structure, corporate culture flows downward. But with the drone/enforcer serving as a de facto firewall, there is a perpetual risk the intended culture (collective values and beliefs) never flows past his domain.

This is why, as the owner, your effort to mentor the drone/enforcer and re-enforce your vision as a "total package that cannot be minimized or compromised or selectively dismantled" is so critically important. In this re-enforcement scenario, the idea of mentoring your second-in-charge is not to brainwash or threaten, but to reveal irresistible truths the drone/enforcer cannot eliminate or refute.

You might have already figured out the other critical building block attached to this strategy. It is simply an undying commitment to stay directly in touch with your employees.

In later chapters, we'll talk about the knowledge-based network system you'll deploy in order to capture the collective knowledge of the organization. Incorporated in that system are mechanisms that facilitate open lines of communication between you and other team members, uncensored by the drone/enforcer or any other go-between. In the end, no one can say their ideas or personal concerns were censored by immediate supervisors, and because of politics or favoritism, never saw the light of day.

Just before the 1986 Space Shuttle Challenger disaster, Roger Boisjoly and Allan McDonald, engineers at Morton-Thiokol, the company that made the solid rocket boosters, express grave concern over launching the Shuttle in extremely cold weather. They had calculated, indisputably, that the cold weather would decrease the elasticity of the synthetic rubber O-rings, which in turn might cause them to seal too slowly and allow hot combustion gas to surge through the joint and cause an explosion.

They reported their findings to Morton-Thiokol management, which, in turn, report it to NASA. Under pressure to launch, NASA's drone/enforcers refused to accept the finding and pressured Morton-Thiokol to revise the calculations. When the two engineers refused to revise their finding, Morton-Thiokol's management revised it for them and sent a watered-down assessment to Jesse Moore, the final decision-maker. Based on the distorted report he received, he gave the green light to launch. The whole crew died because of it.

Had the Anthead System been in place, the two engineers from Morton-Thiokol could've sent the raw report directly to Jesse Moore. There's no guarantee he would've changed his decision. But, at least, the NASA official sitting at the "buck stops here" desk would've understood the total, uncensored ramifications.

Seattle backpack, briefcase, travel bag maker, TOM BIHN, is an excellent example of a small business fully commitment to open, vertical communications with both employees and customers.

The CEO has his own blog where you can communicate directly with him. Designated employees have websites where potential employees can ask uncensored questions about the company's work environment. Customers can query directly about new and existing products.

The drone/enforcer has power, but not absolute power, not with the free flow of information up and down the communications chain. The organization is allowed to grow and reach its potential. Balance is created and sustained by the unobstructed flow of knowledge, keeping a potential communications bottleneck at bay.

Scout

The scout ant is the designated food-finder that ventures outside the mount to located opportunities on which to capitalize. Whether, new or existing food sources, scouts are generally the critical agents of first contact.

In a small business, those sources are called markets; and scouts are the sales personnel. In many ways, scouts represent the lifeblood of the organization. As legendary salesman Arthur H. (Red) Motley put it, *"Nothing happens until somebody sells something."*

The statement has a great deal of merit. There's no capital to invest, no savings to retain and no profit to share. A business might briefly come into existence via an initial bank loans. But someone has to first *sell* the banker on the business concept.

The scout has a crucial responsibility. And, if he or she fails at their job, everything else eventually dies.

One of the most difficult tasks faced by small business owners is hiring competent, effective sales personnel. The primary reason is tied to a previous observation which states owners have a tendency to hire carbon copies of themselves. If you've spent any time working in a sales department, you know salespeople are very, very different from the rest of the herd ... neither, better nor worse ... just different.

Typically, salespeople are extroverts, perpetually optimistic, prone to exaggeration, comfortable with ambiguity, overly flexible with time constraints and resistant to organizational structure. The worst request you can make of a salesperson is to ask him or her to fill out a sales report or make formal forecasts for the upcoming year. For the most part, at least in his mind, bureaucracy, paperwork, long term planning, rigid procedures and research studies are a waste of time.

The scout thrives on the opportunity to close the deal and be justly rewarded for her efforts. But in this hyperactive marketplace, both proportions (closure and reward) are hard to come by.

Consider the spectrum of sales activities from order-taking at the very bottom of the food chain to complex relationship leveraging at the very top. The fierce competition, especially at the top, requires the most effective producers to be innovative in their approach to client solutions, passionate about the products and services they sell, trustworthy to gain repeat business, persistent to ward off rejection, and committed to bringing added value to the process through outstanding service and follow up.

How many salespeople do you know that satisfy those lofty requirements? On the average, 20% of the sales force is responsible for 80% of total sales. That means the 20% have found a groove, or reached a *selling zone* that gives them the advantage over mediocre competition. A scout may go out looking for opportunities. But even when he finds them, the competition may be too sophisticated, too locked in for the new kid on the block to intercede.

As an owner, you want an edge in selecting the most

effective scout your budget can afford. But current sales personality testing offers no consistent correlation between character attributes and ultimate success in the field. Short, dumpy, obnoxious Ralph will hit 100% of his goal, just as tall, charming, soft spoken Bernard hits his. The key is to hire personnel that best reflect the preferences of your prospective customers.

If your company's sales water skis and your key customers have indicated a preference for knowledgeable reps with an outdoors background, it doesn't make sense to send over a fast talking New Yorker in a $700 designer suit, even if he is your best salesman. The key is to hire for your customer, not for yourself.

The second difficulty for scouts in today's marketplace is being justly rewarded for their efforts. The sticking point arises from the vast array of compensation packages in each industry, and the pressure most small business owners are under to sell at a competitive price.

Let's face it. Some owners are greedy and try to keep the profits to themselves. But in most instances, owners have legitimate limitations as to how much they can pay sales personnel and still remain competitive.

If you haven't read *The World Is Flat* by Thomas L. Friedman, you should. It provides some disturbing insight into the global marketplace and how the erosion of America's middle class is not only due to a decade of political favoritism for big business, but also the reduction of living standards based on emerging countries taking advantage of the lightning-fast collaborative technology and using it to snatch away US market share. A factory in India or Brazil or China makes the same product with the same quality for a third of the price. Small businesses in America are caught in the middle.

Seasoned scouts are big thinkers, bold risk-takers and always focused on the end game. Just as Big Mike indicated his disdain for mentoring duties that would take him away from the end game, so it is with the majority of sales personnel. They want to close the deal. And they want to get paid. And if your compensation package is perceived to be unjust or unfair, scouts, especially Xer scouts, will quickly move on to another organization. That translates into additional training costs and a hindrance in your quest for market share.

Under the Anthead System, compensation is key. In order to recruit and retain top-notch producers, you must relegate the order-taking to office clerks. Unleash your salespeople on meaningful key prospects, challenge them with ambitious but realistic sales goals, and to hold on to cream-of-the-crop producers, pay over and above the industry-standard. Many industry associations publish salary and compensation surveys each year. Find out what your competition is doing, and do better.

You also have to be willing to pay scouts for mentoring within the organization. This can come in the form of bonuses, trips, organizational recognition and other perks that scouts consider valuable. This additional compensation can be used to emphasize unity of purpose within the organization and remind scouts they are connected to a bigger process of growing the business as a whole. Forget about the old command-structure, "do it because I say so" mentality. Set clear mentoring and collaboration goals, and pay for results.

A final word on scouts. In their pursuit of the end game, they have a tendency to break the rules. "Tell you what I'm gonna do on this little ole deal. Although you don't qualify, if you promise not to tell anybody...."

A class action lawsuit was filed in Washington State against Pyramid Breweries and its distributor Western Washington Beverage for allegedly conspiring with Service America Corporation, the concessionaire at Safeco Stadium and Seattle Tacoma International Airport concessionaire Host International to circumvent state law. That law mandates that breweries and distributors offer the same pricing to all retailers regardless of quantity. However, Pyramid and Western Washington Beverage allowed the Safeco concessionaire a sweetheart $25-per-keg discount.

In a similar case, British Airways Plc., Deutsche Lufthansa AG and the Air France-KLM Group were among twelve airlines fined $1.1 billion for colluding with competitors on air-cargo, fuel and security surcharges. High-level scouts representing each of these airlines got together in secret and fixed prices to maximize profit for all.

And who can forget the mad rush at the end of 2010 to buy energy efficient doors and windows to get a tax credit of $1500. Slick salespeople lied to thousands of homeowners assuring them they could get the maximum credit as long as they made the purchase by December 31, 2010. In reality, if homeowners didn't have their windows "installed" before January 1st, 2011, by taking the tax credit, they were committing fraud. But what upstanding, go-getter scout was going to miss out on a fat commission by muddying the water with such a minor detail?

Because the Anthead System de-emphasizes hands-on supervision, scouts have a greater opportunity to go astray and cause long-term damage. Your responsibility, along with the drone/enforcer, is to show them in clear terms how their ill-advised actions could bring the whole company down. Your objective is to prick their sense of self-preservation, rather than moral correctness. If there is no company, they don't have a place to work.

Soldier

The soldier ant is the designated protector with a mentality to preserve the integrity of the mound. The soldier fights to the death to keep invaders from without and defectors from within from destroying the community that has been established.

In the Anthead System, it could very well be the security guard at the gate that epitomizes this category of protector. But most often it is the accountants, lawyers and inventory managers that watch over the company's assets to avert any misuse and improprieties.

When you read the story of Tyco's CEO L. Dennis Kozlowski and how he and several associates looted the company of more than $170 million, and obtained $430 million through the fraudulent sale of company shares, you wonder where were the soldiers whose job it was to protect the company. It's one thing to stand on the wall and keep a vigilant eye out for invading forces. It's another to completely turn one's back to the anarchy within.

In the case of Enron, except for one whistle blower by the name of Sherron Watkins, perhaps, the widespread fraud and deceit may have continued for years. Her profile in courage gives us an idea of what kind of soldiers we want to hire for the Anthead System. They should be competent, vigilant, highly ethical and willing to take a stand on unpopular issues.

According to a 2000 labor force poll sponsored by Shell Oil Company, these soldier workers are referred to as Fulfillment Seekers. They want to make the world a better place and seek jobs that allow them to do so. Sounds like a philosophy that would be coveted more by Baby Boomers, than Xers, doesn't it? Most are white, married, and describe themselves as team players rather than leaders. They believed in structure and gravitate away from ambiguity. In their minds, everything should balance out.

Here's the great irony in all of this. The more efficient they are in their roles, the harder yours becomes.

Visionaries, by nature, exist in a futuristic world. They view the present as a resistant stepping-stone leading to the great achievements and discoveries of tomorrow. Visionaries are skilled problem-solvers that exude confidence and seduce our imaginations. Most importantly, they have the ability to inject outlandish possibilities and unproven realities into our heads.

What would you say if the Wright Brothers came to you back in 1902 and ask for a loan because *"people would one day be able to fly"*, or an unknown Donald Trump came to you asking for $100 million to revamp the dilapidated, bankrupted New York Commodore Hotel, claiming he could one day get travelers to pay $800 a night?

If you are an effective, prudent, practical-minded soldier, you would say, "poppycock!" Under the Anthead System, this is what small business visionaries should get used to hearing from their best risk analysts, accountants and financial advisors.

Soldiers see the future, but mostly from the perspective of the mayhem it could bring. What if this goes wrong or that goes wrong, or that Yellowstone great white shark rises up from the Pacific and swallows LA?

These inevitable conflicts represent the chaotic nature of a small business operating under the Anthead System. In pursuing a new idea or concept, you actually "morph" from being an owner (king/queen) to being a salesperson (internal scout). You have to persuade others of the merits of your idea. And if you are unable to sell them on it, you have to make a crucial decision to adhere to their recommendations, or override their advice.

The road gets even bumpier from here.

If you continually override the expertly researched, highly analytical advice of your soldiers, they will eventually stop giving advice at all. They'll deem the entire process a farce, a useless formality with predictable (doing it your way) results. Then why have soldiers in the first place?

Soldiers are valuable cogs in the wheel. They force you to come to the table with your very best ideas. Knowing they will veto any mediocre or flawed concept, you tend to thoroughly research and refine your visionary offerings. You walk into the room thinking, "Okay you skeptical sons-of-#$#@*. You buried my last idea. Try to shoot this one down."

In return, they realize they can't just sit there saying, "we don't like it", or "it too risky", or "no one's tried that before". They'd better have some solid rationale for saying they're against it. Otherwise, get out of the way and let the big wheel of progress roll on.

In the long run, the accumulation of knowledge on potential opportunities will be astounding. We've already talked briefly about the knowledge network system you'll deploy to capture the collective knowledge of the organization. With soldiers drilling down into every hole to find legitimate rationale to pursue or not pursue a visionary strategy, the coffers of knowledge and rich analytics will provide you with strategic advantages in decision-making that will make your competitors cry.

Pick an issue or concept of interest. Now how would you like to go up against Goggle to debate the pros and cons? You already know they're going to eat your lunch because of their superior knowledge base.

Hopefully, you're beginning to recognize a very important reality. Besides human capital, knowledge is an organization's most valuable asset. You may end up successfully revisiting some of your rejected visionary concepts three or four years down the line simply because the collaborative effort between you and your protectors has alerted you, in advance, the time will eventually be right. Movie director James Cameron held on to the *Terminator* script for ten years because his soldiers realistically and prudently informed him the technology to produce the film did not exist.

Soldiers are true assets. Embrace them and their short-sighted perspective in good faith. They will save you a great deal of agony and money in the long run, and make your arsenal of persuasive weaponry better than it's ever been before.

Workers

Worker ants can be divided into two categories: high-tech and low-tech.

High tech ants are responsible for very complex duties that may require highly analytical skills and multitasking. Though low-tech ants are no less important, their duties are generally more redundant in nature.

A good illustration of this delineation of duties is described by University of Toulouse researcher Jerome Orivel and his colleagues in the April, 2005 issue of *Nature*.

In the dense trees of the Amazon, Allomerus worker ants develop a sophisticated trap using a sticky fungus sapling they cultivate from unique body secretions. The trap has galleries or holes just below the surface, where the ants hide, waiting for an insect to land. When an insect lands or sticks, the high tech ants grasp its free legs and stretch the victim across the trap. The low tech ants then swarm out of the holes and sting it to death.

Though members of the group have different functions, they work together as a seamless, overpowering force. But clearly high tech sapling manufacturers have a more tedious calling.

In your organization, high tech knowledge workers such systems analysts, programmers and technicians are called upon to perform critical functions in support of your daily operation. Low tech workers such as receptionist, clericals, delivery drivers and data entry personnel perform important tasks, but tasks that are less likely to be categorized as critical. Furthermore, the two groups approach employment with two totally different perspectives.

Most high-tech employees are high achievers that thrive on the challenge of mastering new gadgetry. Manipulating faster processors, installing computer upgrades, enhancing firewall security, and tweaking software functionality create a sense of career fulfillment and reward for them. Pushing the barriers of technological change is why high tech employees come to work. To keep them happy, you must offer a competitive salary, continuing education and the opportunity to work with updated technology. Otherwise, they "come to work" somewhere else.

In recent years, with a bad economy and more trained technical workers from which to choose, many small businesses are playing a numbers game, hiring too many technical workers, but cutting their hours in order to avoid paying full-time benefits. This also creates a carrot-and-stick scenario providing the owner with the option to reward exceptional workers with more hours and mediocre workers with fewer hours. This may seem like a clever ploy. But in the long run, it creates a sense of resentment and serves as a deterrent to team members taking full ownership of crucial projects.

Remember, these high tech workers are suspicious Xers, more sophisticated in their thinking and more career oriented. It won't take them long to figure out your strategy, and ultimately, come to the conclusion there's no future with your organization.

When you look at a travel company like Expedia with a high turnover rate, you see a composite of many organizations in various industries that employ "profit over people" strategies. Some former employees of the company talk about being misled concerning their true job descriptions and being called out of a meeting to get fired. The toxic environment has already begun to take its toll, facilitating Priceline's effort to take more market share each quarter.

Low tech employees however, sometimes referred to as clock punchers, are less career-oriented, minimally trained and quite often living from check to check. They have a high school diploma, and perhaps, a few hours of college. But generally speaking, their presence within the organization is by chance rather than design. Their primary focus is getting a good performance evaluation which they feel will lead to an incremental increase in salary.

Low tech workers offer an uncultivated opportunity to increase your company's productivity. Most small business owners don't have the time, profiling skills, or serendipity to recognize the untapped contributions low tech workers can provide. With a small amount of training, empowerment and monetary incentive, they are generally eager to pitch in at levels far beyond the constraints of their job description.

Think about how non-medical personnel respond extemporaneously to take care of injured comrades in battle, or ordinary pedestrians pull accident victims out of a burning vehicle. Back in 2008, with just three hours' notice, a 29-year-old understudy, Edward Bennett, only a few years out of the Royal Academy of Dramatic Art, had to step in and take superstar David Tennant's place on stage as Hamlet. He received rave reviews. But before the curtain opened, his hands were shaking so badly, it took ten minutes to tie his shoelaces.

In 1978, San Francisco Mayor George Moscone was unexpectedly assassinated by a rival politician and former member of the City's Board of Supervisors. Current California Senator Dianne Feinstein was forced to take his place as mayor. Overnight it became her responsibility to step up and lead her city out of utter chaos and confusion. She responded magnificently after being placed into an unexpected position of escalated demand.

Each of us has hidden capabilities inside. Sometimes, however, it takes extraordinary circumstances for these capabilities to surface.

Years ago, while working a campaign out of town, I asked my secretary to "morph" into a junior executive, gathering several documents and meeting with two key clients to obtain signatures before a critical deadline. She was petrified. These people were $200,000 a year senior oil executives with silver hair and deep tans and sitting behind $5,000 cherry wood desks. She had to figure out when to smile, went to sit, when to deflect intrusive questions and so on.

She accomplished the task. In fact she did an outstanding job. That Monday morning when she came into work, I had lined her desk with five dollar bills totaling $400. I explained this was something extra for her extra contribution. The increments of five had a special meaning to her because she almost didn't have the five dollars to park in one of the upscale parking garages.

When she realized the extent of my appreciation, she began to cry. After that, she became eager to try new challenging roles within the organization, and eventually moved from secretarial duties to an account services rep.

You'll have low tech workers in your organization willing to stretch their responsibilities. All they're waiting for is the appropriate opportunity. But don't hang them out to dry. Give them the training, encouragement and the reward they deserve. Don't be a sleazy "shuffler" that shuffles off as many extra assignments as possible without compensation. Eventually, workers figure out you're using them and sabotage production or simply leave the company.

Larvae Sacrifice

When we think about the enticing aroma and succulent flavor of grilled shrimp or fried oysters or butter-based lobster, our mouths began to water. But what about ant eggs in the Mexico dish known as *escamoles*, or a paste of the green weaver ants served in Burma as a condiment with curry, or the translucent, sweet taste of North Queensland's blue ants, mashed up in water. Yummy!

The ant species represents a delicacy consumed all over the world. Though not as popular in the United States, ants are considered a safe, reliable source of nourishment, and in some countries, a gateway to spiritual healing.

Most ants go through four distinct growing stages: egg, larvae, pupa and adult. Depending on the environment, care received, and the status of the food supply within the mound, these stages of growth can be altered or even suspended for the sake of the total colony.

The larvae stage is especially remarkable because during this period, these small white, legless globs can eat or be eaten, depending on the state of the community's collective survival. Larvae undergird the tenuous food chain and act as sacrificial lambs that give stability to the colony as a whole.

Under the Anthead System, the larvae sacrifice worker brings a different kind of nourishment to the organization. It's called social consciousness. It's her responsibility to remind the company it exists beyond the context of profit, and is connected to and responsible for society as a whole.

Social consciousness or social responsibility as it is often called is a voluntary moral commitment that goes beyond the window-dressing of donations and charitable contributions to enhance public image. Rather, it is a proactive mindset that embraces organizational conduct designed to fortify the community at large.

Renowned economist Milton Friedman once stated: *"There is one and only one social responsibility of business - to use its resources and engage in activities designed to increase its profits...."*

I believe he relegated the importance of social responsibility to an afterthought rather than incorporating it into the primary scheme of things. He seemed to imply the creation and execution of profit-making strategies are acceptable so long as they don't violate the rules of the game, and that a company's obligations did not extend beyond that pretext.

What are the rules of the game? At one point the rules of the game stated that cigarette companies could develop promotional campaigns explicitly targeting minors; that oil companies could dump harmful by-products into open pits and ditches in foreign countries and then walk away; that logging companies could cut down trees at will with no consideration to the future environmental impact; that chemical plants could continue to pollute the air so long as they were grandfathered in before a certain year's legislation.

Friedman was implying if you stayed within the law and made money, your social responsibility obligations were met.

Amoral organizations allow gray areas and loopholes within the law to drive its moral conduct. "As long as Congress or the Supreme Court or state government hasn't intervened, it must be okay."

But as a small business owner, trying to establish your brand and gain longevity in the marketplace, you should know it's not okay. Enron was giving generously to local charitable organizations. At the same time, it was gouging California consumers with inflated energy prices and hiding the true worth of the corporation from investors. Providian Financial was another company that gave heartily to charities in the front, while cheating credit card holders in the back. In 2001, the organization ended up paying $150 million in fines.

When we look at Ben & Jerry's, however, a founding member of the Business for Social Responsibility (BSR) Association, we see just the opposite approach. For years, Ben & Jerry's has advocated business' central role in pursuing socially conscious practices that improve the quality of life for the community as a whole. The company refers to its socially progressive practices as *"caring capitalism"*, a philosophy which focuses on business ethics, philanthropy, fair treatment of employees, and respect for the environment.

Ben & Jerry's has been recognized by Fortune Magazine as Best Companies for Minorities To Work. The Council on Economic Priorities awarded the company its prestigious Corporate Conscious Award for its socially conscious practices. Working Mother Magazine featured the company as one of the 100 Best Companies for Working Mothers. Co-founders Ben Cohen and Jerry Greenfield personally received the National Retail Federation's American Spirit Award for their social responsibility and participation in community action programs. The list goes on.

The impetus of these achievements flows from the unmitigated belief that social responsibility and maximum profits are not mutually exclusive. An organization can have both. In fact, some studies show being socially responsible actually enhances profits.

Well-known Harvard Business School Professor, Rosabeth Moss Kanter, once said, *"Money should never be separated from values. Detached from values it may indeed be the root of all evil. Linked effectively to social purpose, it can be the root of opportunity."*

As a small business owner, you're not trying to set the philanthropic world on fire. Your objective is to make sure social responsibility is incorporated into your business practices so there is a visible and meaningful advocacy of social consciousness in all of your decision-making. Adopt a sincere policy of social activism, knowing reciprocal benefits such as a positive image in the community, loyal employees, enhanced recruitment capabilities for top talent, and a culture of self-admiration are sure to follow.

When it comes to taking on social consciousness within your organization, larvae sacrifice workers are made to order. They have a heart for the community and a predisposition toward helping others. Adept at volunteering personal time, they are already members of a charitable organization, and at work, instinctively gravitate toward employees in need.

When a larvae sacrifice worker is operating at her best, you hear these statements throughout your organization:

Ms Daily is asking all employees interested in signing up for the blood drive to make sure their name is on the list by Friday.

Ms Daily has arranged car-pooling for all employees whose vehicles were damaged in the flood.

Tomorrow, Ms Daily will be bringing students from the local elementary school to visit our company to see how businesses operate. She is asking everyone to clean up their areas so both students and teachers leave with a positive impression of our company.

As you know, Jacquelyn in accounting lost her mother and father in the tragic tour bus accident this past weekend. Those of you interested in contributing to the funeral arrangements should see Ms Daily by the end of the day.

Ms Daily has arranged a free company-sponsored seafood dinner for all those who participated in the muscular dystrophy bike ride last month. Please see her for details.

You get the picture.

The entire organization feeds off of Ms Daily's kindness and genuine sense of morality. She reinvigorates our belief in the goodness of humankind. This is critically important when you consider how sub-cultures help to influence an organization's dominant culture. If you've ever been in a cut-throat environment, then you know that sub-cultures are the source from which benevolent behavior emerges. There can be a sense of people "helping each other", or as the saying goes, "each man for himself".

The larvae sacrifice worker's official capacity may be creating and distributing the newsletter, press releases, convention packets, and so on. But her true value to the organization is in her reinforcement of an ethical, benevolent, team-oriented organization. Her presence reminds people there is more to life than the obsessive pursuit of profits. In an interconnected world, we must reach out to help each other. This organizational competency of "helping each other" will strengthen your company for the long haul.

Soooooooo, there you have it; your starting lineup for your potential small business dream team: King/Queen, Drone/Enforcer, Scout, Worker (technical and nontechnical), Soldier and Larvae Sacrifice. The number of people in each group will vary, depending on the maturity and strategic direction of your organization.

In the next chapter we'll discuss potential growth strategies for your organization. And you'll be happy to know, the road will smooth out just a bit.

Remember, old management practices are dead or quickly dying out. The Anthead Syndrome is a radical concept, designed to help you survive and prosper in a new, turbulent, hyperactive environment. You'll have to grit your teeth and take deep breaths as you let the old, antiquated practices fall by the wayside. But just as a baby chick sheds its shell to survive and grow, so will you shed your dependency upon a system that no longer works.

Change is not easy, especially when it mandates that you partner with, rather than boss over the people you hired. But if you're still reading at this point, there's hope you can make this necessary transition. Hang in there. You're doing just fine.

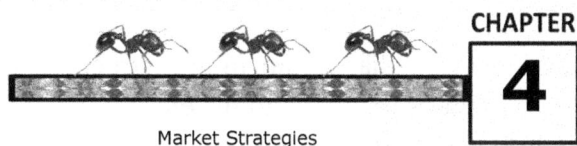

CHAPTER

4

Market Strategies

*W*hat is your purpose for opening a small business? To make money? Sure. And now that you've read the previous chapter, to be a positive agent of social consciousness? Sure. But what is your true mission? What do you plan to do that no one else has done, and if they've done it, how do you plan to do it more effectively?

Here are three mission statements:

- **Wal-Mart:** "To give ordinary folk the chance to buy the same thing as rich people."
- **Google:** "To organize the world's information and make it universally accessible and useful."
- **Blockbuster:** "To be the global leader in rentable home entertainment by providing outstanding service, selection, convenience and value."

In writing this book, my mission was to share my twenty plus years of insight and experience with small business owners in a way that was concise, clear, revolutionary and beneficial to other owners.

Take a look at these three examples from management books that are supposed to assist you in better understanding how to run your business:

Consequent to the failure of the structural and classical form of leadership owing to the emergence of a platform of relations and situational demands, an alternative model is to be practiced.

Concept aims at analyzing the facilitating mechanisms and interdependencies between available resources and innovation outcomes of diverse kinds.

The attribution process is a cause-and-effect analysis which seeks to determine whether a behavior or event is due largely to the situation (external attributions) or personal characteristics (internal attributions).

These were examples of what I absolutely *didn't* want to do. I didn't want small business owners to have to have a dictionary sitting next to them, along with the home number of a tutoring Princeton professor each time they tried to read my book. This was part of my mission.

So what is your mission?

You may have noticed none of these mission statements say, "to make as much money as I can and retire at forty". Rather, the focus is on what value the company will bring to its customers.

Over the years, as a marketing consultant, I've seen companies come and go. Some have no plan to deliver value. Others have a plan, but can't stick to it. Still others have a plan, stick to it and still go out of business because of circumstances beyond their control.

How many VCR manufacturers, video tape rental companies and analogue tape-editing studios followed their plan, built a superior product, gave good customer service, and then when out of business when Blu-Ray and DVD came along? How many mom and pop dry cleaning operations using perchloroethylene were forced out of business because of the Environmental Protection Agency's new regulations on toxic chemicals? According to the National Tooling and Machining Association, because of tight credit and slow or no payment by large auto manufacturers, roughly 15% of all U.S. tooling and machining companies went out of business in 2009.

Let's face it. You can't control everything. What you can control, however, is the strategic execution of your mission. You decide what you want to do, declare it to the marketplace, and then do it based on your strategic plan.

Strategies come in all flavors, too many to name in the scope of this writing. But for the purpose of developing a comparative framework for strategies used in the Anthead System, we will take a look at three of the most popular strategies currently used in today's marketplace.

First, what is a business strategy?

In the simplest of terms, it is the identification of and commitment to a specific course of action intended to make your business grow and prosper. Tyco and Comcast grew with a strategy of acquisitions. Wal-Mart grew with a strategy of lowest price. Apple grew with a strategy of niche innovation.

Popular Market Strategies

Today, the three most popular strategies are: Lowest Cost Provider, Value Differentiator, and Niche Master. Let's take a closer look at all three.

Low Cost Provider

Businesses that adapt a lowest cost provider strategy pursue a competitive advantage and increased market share by providing customers with a "lower" or "lowest" possible price for comparable products and services. Wal-Mart, with net sales of over $405 billion in $2010, is an excellent example of this. So are TigerDirect.com, Acer Computers, JetBlue Airways and India's Tata Motors Nano (A $2,500 vehicle brand new).

Low-cost providers enter a market with the intent of undercutting competitors by offering the essentials of a product or service at a lower price. This is accomplished by reducing the price to a level price-sensitive buyers consider significant and are thereby willing to switch from a competing brand. This price point is usually fluid and somewhat of a juggling act because, in the end, it must be greater than the cost of delivering the product, thus, allowing the merchant to make a profit.

If competitors are selling cell phones for $99 each, and you enter the market with a price of $95, the customer's temptation to switch to your brand at that price is negligible. However, should you drop the price to $49, the chances are much greater the significant difference in price will entice customers to switch.

The problem arises when you realize it costs $50 to manufacture, package, promote and deliver the product. In other words, each time you sell a phone for $49, you lose $1.

This previous scenario is not necessarily a poor strategy, especially if users have to subscribe to your network for $60 per month, or buy a proprietary battery from you that nets $10 per purchase. When the dust clears, you're still making a profit. That's how most cell phone providers are able to give you a $300 phone for free. By the time the two year contract is up, your monthly subscription fees have more than made up the difference.

But most low-cost providers are not satisfied when losses created from bobbing their big head must be made up by wagging their little tail twice as fast. The preferable solution is to make the head pay for itself. In the case of losing a dollar per phone, the cost-saving objective would be accomplished by finding a cheaper wholesale manufacturer offering a lower cost per unit, or finding a more efficient shipping route, or if production is done in-house, finding a way to reduce costs along the value chain.

With the advent of the internet, finding a cheaper wholesaler is now a global proposition. For instance, Dell Computer's build-to-order, just-in-time inventory system receives components from over sixteen different countries on a daily basis. Inventory turnover has been cut down to three days compared to other competitors that average fifteen to twenty days. This reduced inventory cost and the ability to buy new components at rapidly declining prices is just another example of how Dell has gained a strategic advantage.

There are many ways low-cost providers execute strategies to control costs along their value chain. These may include finding cheaper raw materials, installing sophisticated, cost-saving software, negotiating lower labor costs, improving distribution channels and relocating factories to more favorable locations.

The more innovative companies are in managing their costs, the better the chances for success in the marketplace. Overbye

Transport in Lakeville, Minnesota has begun running its trucks on French fry grease to achieve increased gas mileage, cleaner exhaust fumes and a cooler-running engine. Actually, the renewable biodiesel blend is called B20 which has everyday cooking oil as a major component. The WASH ME! Carwash in Kingman, Arizona has installed photovoltaic solar panels on its roof to reduce the monthly electric bill by thirty percent. General Mills, which makes brands like Cheerios and Wheaties, has shrunk the size of its cereal boxes to increase the price per ounce. Management took the chance that customers wouldn't notice or complain. So far, everything seems to be working out.

Using the low costs provider strategy requires an assessment of the market to determine its potential for success. A low-cost strategy works best when competitive products are identical or very similar, target customers are price-sensitive, and switching doesn't carry a significant risk or penalty.

Toothpaste offers a prime example of a product susceptible to a low-cost strategy. Competitors in that industry offer end products that are essentially identical. The bulk of female customers is very price-sensitive. And, there is no penalty for switching between brands.

On the other hand, there is a penalty for breaking a cell phone contract and going to another provider. Furthermore, studies show that early adapters, electronics geeks and business users will snap up new models as soon as they come out, with little consideration for price.

The primary downside to the low cost provider strategy is lost profitability. With razor thin margins, success hinges on increased volume and strict, uninterrupted efficiencies along the value chain. If you enter a mature market where new customers are hard to find, there is the risk that cost-cutting will fail to create a stream of new customers because there are no customers left.

In 1986, roughly 25% of all households in the U.S. owned a

microwave oven. Current estimates hold that over 91% of American households own a microwave oven with an estimated 200 million in use worldwide. If you're targeting the U.S. market with a low costs provider strategy, where are the customers coming from to give you the volume you need to offset lost margins? In addition, if anything unexpected happens to drive up costs along your value chain, you have no room to recover.

Ever wonder why the waitress keeps coming over to your table asking if you want anything else? If the restaurant is built on a low cost provider strategy, profitability is based on the high turnover of each table, meaning the longer you sit there tying up a table, sipping on coffee, the greater the chances are the dollar volume assigned to that table will not be realized. Perhaps, the table needs to turn twenty meals a day at an average cost of $18 per meal, and there you are reading the newspaper and mulling over a two dollar cup of coffee. Somebody please pull the fire alarm.

The lesson here is simple. Study the market thoroughly to see if the low cost provider strategy is appropriate for your product or service. If it is, dive in, but only with the understanding that as the market matures, the strategy will no longer be effective and must be phased out for a more attribute-driven approach.

Value Differentiator

In his 1933 book, *Theory of Monopolistic Competition*, Harvard economist Edward Chamberlin defined product differentiation as the process of distinguishing a product or offering from others, to make it more attractive to a particular target market. This involves differentiating it from competitors' products as well as a firm's internal lineup of similar products.

In more contemporary terms, differentiation is the pursuit of a marketing strategy that emphasizes the unique qualities of one product or service over another. Sometimes the difference is more perceived than real, as in the widespread belief the exact same blend of gasoline from Exxon is superior to that of a small town independent convenience store. Perceived or real, the ultimate goal is to have potential customers act on their beliefs.

Differentiation seeks to make a product or service more appealing by favorably contrasting its unique attributes with competing products or services, thereby gaining a competitive advantage. Most often, this is achieved by establishing a difference in quality, a difference in features, functionality and/or design, a difference in distribution, a difference in availability, and, of course, a difference in price.

Netflix differentiated itself through availability, method of delivery and price. Lexus differentiated itself through quality, product design, groundbreaking value-added customer service and price. Michelin differentiated itself through reliability. Walgreens, choosing not to go head-to-head with Wal-Mart and other retailers on price, differentiated itself through convenience, ease of parking, speed of checkout, and dynamic technological solutions such as self-service photographic output and an online pre-ordering system to enhance transfer of prescriptions.

A strategy of *perceived* differentiation can easily be seen in luxury markets. Celebrity endorsers such as Elizabeth Taylor, Michael Jordan, Christina Aguilera and Usher stand in front of the camera, telling customers a certain perfume or cologne smells better than all of the rest; that it will enhance the viewer's social life and make him or her the "winner" their personal, lifelong accomplishments have failed to do. Research shows this personal stamp of approval goes a long way to justify the $150 per bottle the customer has to pay. Style-conscious, brand-driven consumers seek reinforcement of their personal status through product association. These customers perceive real value in being associated with certain lifestyle brands.

Sometimes a ridiculously high price elevates the sense of value, especially with abstract products such as paintings and antiques. The *Mona Lisa* has the highest insurance value for all painting, a whopping $713 million. I suppose it would be useless to tell them this is just a dead man's paint on a decaying canvas.

Differentiation can also be achieved through creating a mystique or sense of exclusivity. At one point Bernie Madoff, the infamous architect of the largest Ponzi schemes in the history of Wall Street, put out the word he was no longer taking on clients, no matter how much money they had. With that announcement came a tidal wave of investors, beating down his door. People were using their inside connections with friends and associates to plead with Mr. Madoff to make an exception and take them on as a new client.

In 2009, customers camped outside stores to get their hands (and feet) on the new limited edition Space Jam Air Jordan tennis shoes for the meager offering of $175 per pair. The same buying frenzy surrounded the release of the Xbox 360 console and the slim-line PlayStation 2. And who could forget the Cabbage Patch Kid with sales exceeding $600 million back in 1985.

The idea of belonging to an exclusive group has power. Country club members, yacht club enthusiasts and participants in secret fraternal orders attest to this willingness to spend money on an intangible sense of exclusivity. The reality of its value is in the mind of the cardholders.

Providing a more explicit view of differentiation in their *McKinsey Quarterly* business journal article, *When Your Competitor Delivers More For Less,* Robert J. Frank, Jeffrey P. George, and Laxman Narasimhan revealed a noteworthy limitation to this strategy. They explained:

"To compete with value-based rivals, mainstream companies must reconsider the perennial routes to business success: keeping costs in line, finding sources of differentiation, managing prices effectively. Succeeding in value-based markets requires infusing these timeless strategies with greater intensity and focus, and then executing them flawlessly. Differentiation, for example, becomes less about the abstract goal of rising above competitive clutter and more about identifying opportunities left open by the value players' business models."

The critical point they're trying to make is not all differentiation matters. The key to success is to study the marketplace to determine whether major competitors have left gaps in their product or service strategy. Secondly, you must determine whether these gaps actually matter to consumers.

If you own a tractor company and decide to differentiate along the lines of color, will it make a significant difference to farmers whether they are driving a blue one or red one or yellow one?

In order for a differentiation strategy to work, the difference in your product must be valued by the end user. One of the most common pitfalls in executing a differentiation strategy is investing time and money into product differences that mean nothing to customers. Should you put a gold-plated handle on your tennis rackets or force your delivery drivers to sing a cheerful song each time they deliver a package, or give each blend of motor oil a different scented smell? If it doesn't matter to your customers, then it will have no impact on their buying decision. In the long run, you end up increasing costs, eroding profits, and touting differences that weaken your image.

When Southwest Airlines first eliminated their on-board meals, in exchange for peanuts, pretzels and drinks, market analysts speculated whether the absence of such a traditional amenity would cause the airline to lose customers. As it turned out, the meal as a differentiation tool was not as important as the significantly lower prices the airline provided. In other words, considering all aspects of the purchase, the meal didn't matter.

It's also important to evaluate the intrinsic nature of a product or service to determine whether it lends itself to a differentiation strategy. Some products or services such as hotels and cell phones are excellent candidates because of the wide diversity of usage. Customers seek hotels for a variety of reasons including business or vacation travel accommodations, conventions and seminars, weddings and parties, or simple social outlets (bars) at the end of a hard day at the office. With cell phones, senior citizen customers may need only to call relatives, while business executives demand a device that will function as a mobile office. There are also college students that seek lightning fast downloads and access to social networks.

These differentiation opportunities are in contrast to products such as paper clips or marshmallows or chalkboard erasers, where usage is limited with little opportunity to add meaningful bells and whistles. In these situations, low cost providers have a greater prospect of dominating the market than do value differentiators.

In the final analysis, value differentiation requires a trial and error approach that can pay handsome dividends if your product extras are meaningful to customers. Apple keeps leaving competitors behind with innovation and differentiation that means something to potential buyers. Movie studios keep budgeting in director Steven Spielberg's five extra camera angles because it apparently means something to viewers.

So it is with your product or service. Find what customers care about and use this critical knowledge to set your offering apart from everyone else's.

Niche Master

Just as the name implies, niche masters pursue specific market clusters or subsets with the intent of dominating or mastering the needs of customers within that niche. This is accomplished through strategies that focus on price points, quality and reliability, features and functionality, geographic location and availability, and any other value-added attribute that appeals to that specific market.

Mastering the needs of the market carries with it a sense of authority about the company's ability to identify and satisfy the target customer's hierarchy of needs. In most instances, a niche master such as Apple or Southwest Airlines controls a dominant share of the market and is viewed as the trendsetter or market leader in that particular category. Protecting its dominant share requires constant vigilance of marketplace challengers, and acting with speed and decisiveness to shore up any known or perceived weaknesses.

eBay, under attack from a growing number of auction-related competitors, dropped its own Billpoint online payment service and bought PayPal for an estimated $1.5 billion. The acquisition helped to speed up the payment process for customers, the majority of whom had shown a preference for PayPal over Billpoint, and gave eBay a more long-term, dominate position in the marketplace. Conventional brick-and-mortar tax preparation service, H&R Block, continuing to lose online market share to Intuit's TurboTax, purchased online tax-prep software TaxACT for an estimated $287 million. These, along with other highly publicized acquisitions, are indicative of an organization's effort to shore up perceived competitive weaknesses. Though appearing to be very costly investments, in the long run, inaction, as demonstrated by Blockbuster, would cost even more.

Understanding the difference between a value differentiator and a niche master can be a bit confusing. In reality, they both seek niches to pursue and control. The difference between the two essentially comes down to the size of the market and the general preference of attack. Here are several examples.

Most people who shower or bathe use some type of soap. The market is huge. But what Unilever's Dove does is appeal to the total market using a differentiation strategy. It calls its soap a beauty bar with moisturizing cream. That positioning is obviously directed at women who, by the way, epitomizes the dominate decision-maker in terms of which soaps come into the household. You could say they are going after the woman's niche. But really that group (women) is too broad to be called a niche. Dove is actually pursuing the broad market using a differentiation strategy that appeals to the prime purchaser.

Now let's look at that same market from the prospective of a niche master. Dermisil Medicated Ringworm Soap is designed to eliminate ringworms without harsh chemical treatments. With this product, soap-maker Dermisil is pursuing a specific niche with a certain ailment or condition. The target group is much smaller and seeking a product to address a specific need.

The same holds true for Rainbow Depot and 10percent. com, retailers that specialize in clothing for gay men. Just as JoS. A Bank Clothiers, Macy's and the Men's Wearhouse sell men's clothing, so do they. But their niche is small and tied to a specific lifestyle. They are not trying to compete in the broad marketplace.

For years, regional craft beers across the U.S. have pursued a niche strategy to survive. Unable to compete head-to-head with major beer companies such as Budweiser, Miller and Coors, regional craft beers have learned to expand market share based on taste, location and ole school appeal.

There's Headwrecker and P-Stock out of Boston, still pushing its 64-ounce container strategy, Gansett in New England, extremely popular through a conscientious effort of aligning itself with Red Sox fans, Yuengling in Pennsylvania, churned out by the oldest brewery in the United States, Old Style in Chicago, tightly associated with, and for sixty years, sponsor of the Chicago Cubs, and Shiner in San Antonio, a lasting symbol of Texas pride. These regionals have demonstrated a staying power that simply eludes most marketing rationale. Somehow, they've carved out a place in the hearts of their narrow, eclectic customer base and found a way to prosper and grow.

Progressive Insurance offers another example of a niche master, successfully carving out a subset of the huge car insurance market. Rather than trying to compete across the wide spectrum of potential policy owners, Progressive has developed a strategy that caters to high-risk drivers with accidents and traffic violations, motorcyclists, teens, and other traditionally undesirable policy holders. These drivers offer better margins and are willing to pay higher rates. Because of the high premiums and overall company-friendly policies, Progressive is still able to make a healthy profit.

Niche Master Rules

Under the Anthead System, niche masters follow four basic rules:

Rule 1

Choose a market that's large enough to support fragmentation. Otherwise, a limited customer base will create more head-to-head competition, reduce margins, and eliminate the incentive to invest in a comprehensive program that drills down deeply to meet the needs of customers. Segmented marketing is expensive, time-consuming and hard to justify if, in the end, the target population is too small to produce substantial dividends.

Rule 2

Choose a market with substantial barriers to entry. This reduces the number of challengers possessing the financial and technical resources necessary to become a player in the game. Most companies are unable to open an automobile factory or hotel or biotech business overnight. They may see a gap in your strategy, but don't have the resources to take advantage of it. Conversely, if you open a fruit stand on the corner and demonstrate the consistent ability to make a profit, competitors will spring up all around you.

Having said that, the deeper your vertical integration into a market, the harder it is to get out when and if the market dies. As a reference, vertical integration is a hierarchy of companies or operations under the same or closely related ownership, controlling both upstream suppliers and downstream distributors, and working in coordination to satisfy a common need. The Carnegie Steel Company is an excellent example of successful vertical integration. The company owns iron ore and coal mines, the ships and trains that carry the coal, and the factories that processed the raw materials. If a new fuel source suddenly came out to replace coal, it would be very difficult for the company to get out of the business.

Dell, however, is the shining star of horizontal integration across various markets and suppliers. Remember how nimble they operate with total just-in-time (JIT) inventory turnover in three days. They are able to take advantage of price reductions and component updates almost immediately. They can also redeploy resources with lightning speed when a market is tapped out.

A vertical integration strategy gone bad can be seen in the circumstances surrounding military niche supplier, Loral Rolm MIL-Spec. Company executives watched its annual sales plummet from a \$100 to \$50 million and 1,100 employees dwindle to 150 when its MIPS Systems RISC chip for a rugged military workstation was replaced by a newer, more efficient chip made by Sun Microsystems. Heavy investment in vertical manufacturing locked the company into a noncompetitive position against its newly arrived competition.

Barriers can also be established in the form of patents and copyrights. Big pharmaceutical companies such as Pfizer and Merck gain exclusive monopolies on drugs they have developed and had approved by the Food and Drug Administration. Copy-cat competitors are restricted from selling generic versions of these drugs for a designated period of time as with Pfizer's popular cholesterol treatment, Lipitor, which earned Pfizer in excess of \$10 billion a year in protected sales since 1997. This type of barrier is a significant cornerstone to the company's overall marketing strategy. Even when the patent runs out, the upstream R&D labs that created the drug remain a vital part of the company's effort to develop other drugs with the same profit potential.

As a small business owner, you want barriers in the marketplace. You just don't want them to be insurmountable to your operation. Search for the balance that fits your strategic capability. Then, don't be afraid to dive right in.

Rule 3

Choose a market that is still growing and not yet mature. A mature market has generally reached a state of equilibrium when the market is saturated by suppliers, there is little or no product innovation and demand has been overrun by supply. A good example would be modems and connectors. As the tech market moves to high speed and wireless functionality, many old accessories such as adapters and connector cables are in a state of flux; not quite obsolete, but certainly not worthy of investing marketing dollars nor time and energy in innovation. Third world countries might use these products for a bit longer. But everyone knows the writing is on the wall. The marketplace, as well as most of the products that so diligently served it, will soon be history.

A growth market is one that's blossoming in the early stages of its life cycle with predictable opportunity for years to come. The off-the-shelf reading glasses market provides a viable example of this. Over fifty million Baby Boomers will be moving into retirement by 2014. With most suffering from presbyopia (old eye), a vision condition involving the loss of the eye's ability to focus on close objects, the market is ripe for opportunistic competitors with an effective differentiation plan.

Though Magnivision, with numerous of styles and different magnification powers, is currently the market leader, Zoom Eyeworks Inc and Longs Drug Stores Corp are eroding Magnivision's dominant market position with hard-hitting ad campaigns promoting attributes of functionally, shape, color, and fashion appeal. This is precisely what the fashion-conscious, never-get-old Baby Boomers want to hear.

Notice, I said a *differentiation* plan. Pursuing a niche with a differentiation strategy is common. However, competitors entering the market could've easily pursued that same niche with a low cost provider strategy. And yet, we call them niche masters because, unlike Dove, they are NOT pursuing the broad "vision" market in total, but have carved out a Baby Boomer subset of which they intend to master the customer's needs.

Conditions in the off-the-shelf reading glasses market are perfect for a small business operating under the Anthead System. The market is expanding. No single company or brand has an insurmountable market share, which means customers are still open to new avenues of appeal. The product offers multiple opportunities to increase value by adding attractive bells and whistles. Finally, the barriers to market entry are substantial but not formidable. Not every business has the capital or technology to open an eyeglass factory. However, the barriers are manageable and do not compare to the headaches of opening, for example, a nuclear plant.

Rule 4

Choose a market that is compatible with your organization's unique competencies. This means pursuing a product or service niche which matches your passion and interests, as well as those of your employees. This is so important and requires an extended discussion.

A lifestyle tradition for many females from the Baby Boomer generation was to curl up in front of the fireplace with a good book, eagerly preparing for the chance to discuss the characters and plot with other avid readers and friends. Today, however, most internet-driven Xers and Millennials are less inclined to read long documents. They run from offerings such as Leo Tolstoy's 1400-page novel, *War and Peace*. And their "short" reading is done on an iPhone or Kindle.

With an employee lineup of Xers and Millennials, it wouldn't make good business sense to open a bookstore. No one would want to engage in the fundamental task of reading, maybe, a short romance or two. No one would have a passion for the product. It would be the same as putting an old Traditionalist behind the counter in an AT&T phone store, or trying to get Xers to sell cigarettes. The employees in the organization need to match the niche you intend to pursue.

The selection of a niche, however, goes far beyond the generational tendencies of employees. Besides evaluating your company's time, money, equipment, supplies, contacts and previous specializations, it's important to have some idea of the "stretch value" or "morphing capability" of key areas of operations. This important assessment points to your organizational competencies.

In a traditional environment, most management systems attempt to identify organizational competencies by having the human resources department or an internal focus group list the top five characteristics and traits that typify successful employees within the organization. From that point, an emphasis is placed on hiring new employees that exemplify these traits, while simultaneously mentoring current employees to adapt these practices.

If you're just starting your business, there's a very good chance you don't even have a human resources department, or a manager with a clear understanding of what you're trying to accomplish. As the king/queen, the responsibility of identifying your organizational competencies falls strictly upon your shoulders. Remember what President Harry S. Truman's sign read: *"The Buck Stops Here."*

Although it may seem like a daunting task, under the Anthead System, it's really quite straightforward. In the previous chapter, we already identified the type of workers you're going to need: King/Queen, Drone/Enforcer, Scout, Worker (technical and nontechnical), Soldier and Larvae Sacrifice. Now, it's just a matter of making sure these key contributors possess the core competencies necessary for your organization to succeed.

Remember, you're trying to evaluate your company's organizational competencies as they relate to the niche you intend to pursue. But under the Anthead System, you will be pursuing multiple niches, sometimes, simultaneously. Your organization will be "morphing" from niche to niche based on the range of opportunities you've determined most compatible with your unique organization.

Many of you are football fans. You'll recall, in the old days, the quarterback would summon his team together in the huddle, call a play, and then come up to the line of scrimmage to execute the play. Today, the quarterback might not even call a play in the huddle, but rather, line up at the line of scrimmage, evaluate the defense, and then call a play based on the range of options his team has pre-determined would best succeed against that particular defensive formation.

There are two things to consider here. First, it's not just the quarterback calling the play, but the offensive coordinator on the sidelines, the team's scout who has watched the opponent in advance, and the quarterback who has also studied the films and understands the strengths and weaknesses of both his team and the opposing team. In other words, each play, that is, each attempt to exploit an opportunity, is a collaborative effort. Secondly, the entire effort exists in a state of flux or ambiguity until the decision is made on which play will actually be run.

So it is with your small business under the Anthead System. The decision on which niche to pursue will be a collaborative effort. Remember, you'll have to sell your team on your visionary ambitions? Secondly, the company's primary focus will remain in a state of flux from year to year, based on the distribution of current resources and the niche opportunities that unfold at a particular time.

In larger companies, Wall Street refers to this as a "strategic retreat" or "shedding unprofitable business units" or redeploying company resources". These are code phrases that suggest a company has decided to take its money out of one market and invest it into another market that has more promise for its culture and competencies.

It's important to understand there may very well be nothing wrong with the market, itself. Rather, the company has determined that, going forward, it's not a fit for that particular line of business.

Korean electronics giant Samsung sold its hard drive

business to Seagate. The deal gave Samsung a much needed infusion of capital, about $1.4 billion in cash and stock, while bumping Seagate's global market share up to 40%. The Lenovo Group jumped into the mobile phone business, then jumped back out, selling its mobile phone handset unit to a group of investor and realigning strategic emphasis on its core PC business.

What is General Electric, the maker of refrigerators, electric ranges and gas cooktops, doing owning NBC television and Universal Studios Home Entertainment? The answer is quite simple. They seek out all opportunities within their range of organizational competencies.

In evaluating your small business, there are five baseline competencies you want to establish and hire for within your organization. They are:

- flexibility
- integrity
- analytical thinking
- innovative thinking
- appreciative inquiry

Everything else will remain in a state of flux.

The need for flexibility is quite obvious. The United States military has moved from a large contingent of combat soldiers to smaller, more flexible strategic strike units, as used in the assault on the Osama bin Laden compound, with the capability to respond to a crisis anywhere in the world. In a hostile, unpredictable environment, rapid deployment is everything. Yet, not all soldiers are suited for these kinds of ambiguous, highly mobile, ever-evolving assignments.

The same holds true for your organization. Some employees are just not compatible with an environment driven by rapid change and a built-in mandate to constantly adapt. These employees will not fare well under the Anthead System. They seek the comfort of structure, and rebel when it is taken away.

This potential conflict with the traditional, highly structured business approach can easily be addressed during the hiring process. As the owner, you must emphasize to the point of redundancy how different your organization is going to be. By doing so, applicants are given the opportunity to buy in or out of the process before they come onboard.

The need for high integrity is also obvious. If you've ever had the opportunity to be a part of a self-directed work team, you already understand the importance of integrity. A self-directed work team (SDWT) is a group of employees who combine their unique skills and talents to accomplish a common goal or task without traditional managerial supervision. These employees set priorities, work schedules and desired outcomes based on the company's mission statement, core values and profit expectations. There are no time clocks and nobody's standing over their shoulder. They are empowered to find innovative ways to get the job done more efficiently, and in the process, assume the role of risk takers, using company funds.

Under the Anthead System, there are many instances where the employee works without direct supervision, gathering information, studying trends, compiling reports and recommendations, negotiating with external providers and seeking new sources of revenue. Unless the employee is self-driven with a strong work ethic, there could be a tendency to hide in the ambiguity of constant role-changing and re-prioritizing. You'll eventually find out, but it might take some time. The best solution is to hire employees that thrive on goal attainment and positive results.

Analytical thinking is defined as separating or pulling apart distinguishing elements of a concept or problem in order to understand its inner workings. In comparison, innovative thinking is the radical departure from a traditional or accepted approach, with the intent of creating value. Under the Anthead System both are essential because the general impetus is to totally dissect an existing product or process and create something better.

The deep waters of analytical thinking could easily drown us if we ventured out too far. But, because it is so critical to the success of a small business operating under the Anthead System, it is essential we take a momentary plunge.

Analytical thinking entails dissecting or separating out parts of a product or process. But analytical thinking is incomplete without synthetical thinking which studies how all parts work together as a whole. The two thinking methodologies work hand-in-hand to provide insight into the complex systems that influence the collective marketplace.

Let's say we discover in the U.S. recreational market, because of retiring Baby Boomers, camping and hunting activities are growing by 30% per year. In seeking a niche marketing opportunity, we discover both campers and hunters are unhappy with the selection of flashlights used doing critical nighttime activities. We use analytical thinking to dissect the attributes of the top-selling flashlights to discover most are fragile, cheap metal cylinders that cannot be dropped or banged or subjected to any kind of heavy impact without damaging the circuitry and rendering the light inoperable.

In this investigative phase of analytical thinking, we also discover it's not just the cheap metal housing around the circuitry creating a problem, but the cheap circuitry, itself. The housing is imported from China, the circuitry from Viet Nam. Existing competitors seem to be using a low cost strategy, competing almost exclusively on price. You suspect there might be a differentiation opportunity for a high-end, durable, long-lasting flashlight. Perhaps, you can become the Lexus of that product category. You dream of a superior line of flashlights called "Big Bright".

Through innovative thinking, your company comes up with a new design that improves the circuitry components and places them in the center of the cylinder, protected by a hard, rubber enclosure. Your new design also replaces the cheap metal housing with a sturdy, lightweight, non-corrosive titanium outer shell.

Now here's where synthetical thinking comes in.

After thoroughly testing the prototype, and developing a final plan for marketing and distribution, your primary product manager walks into your office with an article on titanium. The article states that titanium dioxide has recently been classified by the International Agency for Research on Cancer (IARC) as an IARC Group 2B carcinogen possibly carcinogenic to humans. The test results show that high concentrations of pigment-grade (powdered) and ultrafine titanium dioxide dust caused respiratory tract cancer in rats exposed by inhalation and intratracheal instillation.

Oh hell no!!!

You can already see your competitors running ads and sending out tons of emails saying, "Don't use Big Bright flashlights. They'll give you cancer."

Of course, titanium dioxide dust is completely different from your titanium flashlight casings. But who's going to take time to listen to that message?

You've put a proficient, compatible team in place, discovered a very promising niche, developed a superior product and created a winning marketing strategy. But synthetical thinking alerts you that all parts of the marketplace equation ... economic, techno-logical, social and political ... have an impact on your ultimate success or failure. In this case, the social impact points overwhelmingly to potential failure.

Your saving grace is that you have the right team in place to either overcome your product vulnerability or find a new niche entirely. This is why building your organizational competencies on a strong foundation of analytical and innovative thinking is so critical. If the team can't find a viable substitute for the titanium, you simply "morph" to the next promising niche.

It's a smart idea to develop analytical thinking within your organization prior to a crisis. At Google, engineers are allowed to spend twenty percent of their time or one day per week on projects that aren't necessarily in their job descriptions. They can develop something new, or if something is broken or incomplete, they can use the time to work on it. The process encourages both analytical and innovative thinking and, through the use of company time and resources, empowers the employee to take substantive action that will benefit the organization over the long haul.

Finally, in the building blocks of organizational competencies, is Appreciative Inquiry.

In her book, *The Thin Book of Appreciative Inquiry*, Sue Hammond explains:

"The traditional approach to change is to look for the problem, do a diagnosis, and find a solution. The primary focus is on what is wrong or broken; since we look for problems, we find them. By paying attention to problems, we emphasize and amplify them. Appreciative Inquiry suggests that we look for what works in an organization. The tangible result of the inquiry process is a series of statements that describe where the organization wants to be, based on the high moments of where they have been. Because the statements are grounded in real experience and history, people know how to repeat their success."

Appreciative Inquiry is essentially a change management process based on the premise that in every organization something works effectively and change can be managed through the identification of what works. This nontraditional way of thinking probes a company's best attributes and practices, and transfers the identifiable processes to other parts of the operation.

Appreciative Inquiry is generally introduced to an organization using the four-D model:

- **Discovery**
- **Dream**
- **Design**
- **Destiny**

Discovery

Employees meet formally with each other in a structured environment to share true stories about the organization and discover times when it performed at its best. If your organization is new, you may not have many stories to tell. But you can use inspiring substitute accounts such as the rise to prominence of other small companies like Apple who no one gave a fighting chance to succeed. As the owner, you can talk about your struggles to get the company started and how your few employees can in and made a difference.

Dream

Employees are encouraged to envision the organization as if the high performance moments previously identified in the "discover" phase are the rule, at all times, rather than the exception. What would it be like if everyone pulled together the same way they did that weekend during the flood when people came into the office and worked nonstop until all the orders were shipped out? In many ways, participants are bringing the best parts of the past forward to formulate new, positive realities.

Design

A select team of employees is empowered to design a working model of the collective dreams the organization has explored during the previous session. This initial plan is embellished by the entire group until it is a practical fit for your organization. Practical means affordable and attainable; otherwise the process will be deemed a useless exercise in futility.

Destiny

This final phase involves the actual implementation of the changes. We step boldly into a reality we have created though re-thinking our relationships to the organization, stakeholders and the community as a whole. The new processes are closely monitored and revamped as needed.

Green Mountain Coffee Roasters used Appreciative Inquiry to reduce its operating costs by 25 cents per pound of coffee. Roadway Express reduced its fourth quarter turnover by 25%. John Deer improved product cycle time and saved $3 million, with more cost saving projected over time. They entered a dream state of possibilities, exploring what could be, and then refusing to accept the notion it couldn't be.

What if we could go to the moon? Somewhere along the way, we discovered that only our restricted imagination was holding us back. So it is with your small business. If you can dream it and believe it, you can find a way to make it happen.

We began this chapter developing a clear, concise mission, followed by the examination of competitive strategies that were compatible with your unique organization. You probably noticed the inordinate amount of time spent on niche marketing. That's because, with a startup business or one still in its infancy, niche marketing gives small businesses operating under the Anthead System the best possible chance for success. It's not to say the low cost provider or differentiator strategy is any less effective. But with limited capital and a small number of employees, it's best to use those strategies inside a particular niche.

In our next chapter, we'll talk about the information necessary to identify a niche and formulate a plan to exploit it. We'll also examine the technological tools that facilitate our effort. Remember. Just because a niche exist doesn't mean it's compatible with your small business team. Know your organizational competencies. And then, move forward to match those opportunities with what your organization does best.

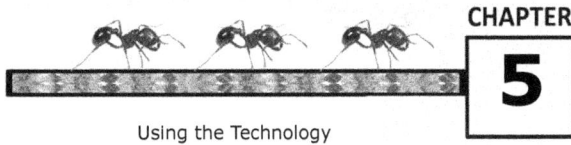

CHAPTER

5

Using the Technology

*T*hroughout our quest to fine niche opportunities, we have drawn upon multiple sources of market data to support our decision-making and restrain our choices to a more metric-driven perspective. You might have wondered where all of this information comes from and whether it's available to your organization.

In this new internet-driven information age, there are literally thousands of sources of useful marketing and management data, free to anyone wanting to use it, or, if not free, available at a price. The fact is most managers are drowning in data. A 2010 SAS/Leger Marketing survey revealed that 47% of Canadian executives felt the amount of information they had overwhelmed them to the extent that daily decision-making was actually impeded by the availability of too much irrelevant information that pulled the manager away from the business at hand.

While writing this book I found myself seduced by some extraordinary findings which had nothing to do with the subject matter I had set out to research. Luckily, the boss (my wife) wasn't nosing around to catch me goofing off.

The point is the fascinating, ever-evolving dikes of commerce that surround the marketplace are overflowing with information. The challenge is to capture, compile, sort, evaluate, and act upon the information in a useful way.

In this chapter, we'll address that epic challenge. How do we exploit critical knowledge to reach our small business goals?

Information Resources

Using a simplistic approach to a very complex topic, we divide the information into two categories: internal and external. Sometimes there is overlapping. But for the most part, the information will come from inside your company (internal), or from outside sources (external) that have already gathered the data, or agreed to conduct some type of research study or survey to accommodate your specific needs.

Let's begin with some of the heavy-hitters:

- **Nielsen Company** ... a global information and media company, supplying marketing and media information, TV ratings, online intelligence, mobile measurement, and analysis of marketplace dynamics and consumer attitudes and behavior.

- **Simmons Market Research Bureau** ... provides annual audience composition information about print media and national television viewing; also provides transactional information about the spending behavior of consumers.

- **Audit Bureau of Circulations** ... a forum of leading publishers, advertisers and advertising agencies providing trusted, verified media buying information, as well as an array of free and subscribed-to readership, subscriber demographics and online activity data.

- **National Opinion Research Center (NORC)** ... a University of Chicago campus social research organization providing government agencies, non-profit agencies and corporations national survey data related to society and culture, economics and population, and education and child development.

- **Goliath** ... an online research center offering corporate profiles, market reports, and business leads on over 400,000 private companies worldwide. The company also offers over 3 million articles, with new articles fed into the database each day.

- **Forrester Research** ... an independent technology and market research company that provides best practices and analysis of issues and trends impacting Information & Knowledge Management and Infrastructure & Operations professionals.

- **Starch Research** ... employing benchmark marketing and public opinion surveys, Starch provides advertisers with proof of advertising effectiveness.

- **Audits & Surveys Worldwide Inc** ... provides marketing research & public opinion polling services, mail surveys, marketing analysis, service trade statistics, and commodity price forecasting.

- **Radius Global Market Research** ... provides a range of innovative research products and approaches to address critical issues in development, marketing and communications.

- **Arbitron** ... provides survey research information to help radio stations, television stations and streaming media businesses evaluate audiences and create better programming for their listeners and viewers.

- **Cogent Research** ... provides custom marketing research, syndicated research products, and evidence-based consulting to leading organizations in the financial services, life sciences and consumer goods industries.

- **Nielsen Claritas SiteReports** ... offer the most accurate online source for U.S. demographics and is the first to offer current year and five year demographic projections.

- **A Fresh Green Perspective** ... is a monthly sustainability-focused subscription service that includes a broad-based overview and the ability to select custom reports on over 70 topics tailored to an organization's particular needs. The service was created to help businesses, organizations and government agencies examine topics most significance to their business.

Of course, there are many more reputable paid or subscription-based research companies available. The source or sources you ultimately select will depend on the complexity of need, the type of business you're in, the niche you've decided to pursue, and the budget you're willing to expend.

In many cases, the information is free if you know where to look. There are numerous online forums, industry associations and charitable funded websites that track statistical data about their industry as a service to members. A good example is the American Cancer Society's website: www.cancer.org. On the very first page, it states:

"Breast cancer is the most common cancer among American women, except for skin cancers. The chance of developing invasive breast cancer at some time in a woman's life is a little less than 1 in 8 (12%). The American Cancer Society's most recent estimates for breast cancer in the United States are for 2010:

- About 207,090 new cases of invasive breast cancer will be diagnosed in women.

- About 54,010 new cases of carcinoma in situ (CIS) will be diagnosed (CIS is non-invasive and is the earliest form of breast cancer).

- About 39,840 women will die from breast cancer.

Perhaps, you're searching for basic information to support your company's annual cancer drive. This would be an excellent starting point.

Another example would be consumerREVIEW.com. This site is a leading source of user-generated buying advice for outdoor sporting goods and consumer electronics. Though the site is a bit slow and clunky, thousands of consumers visit to learn, interact, and buy products showcased within their network of web communities.

Here's an arbitrary consumer review of the Sony DSC-F828 Cybershot camera posted in one of the forums:

"Canons S95 has a wide aperture that is especially useful for indoor, close-up photos. The Sony DSC-R1 is the next logical step beyond the f-828, it is built very similar, but has a full size APS sensor and an outstanding Zeiss lens. That camera would produce better detail than any of the others we are talking about by a significant amount. But I digress, I'd like to hear why the F-828 is not sufficient for your needs. That's a very solid camera and replacing it will be difficult because those are big shoes to fill."

Contributors in other forums happened to agree with this assessment. Thus, if I were buying or considering marketing a competitive camera, this would give me an idea of current attitudes within the marketplace.

The Expert Exchange (http://www.experts-exchange.com/) is a technology help website offering specialized expertise from real people around the globe. The annual access subscription fee is about $100, but well worth the investment.

JustAnswer is another expert advice website. You simply choose the type of expert you need (lawyer, doctor, plumber, technician, etc) and then type in your question. Competing experts will offer you an answer and a price for you to accept or reject.

For the current state of global warming, green earth initiatives, renewable energy legislation, and green business growth and prosperity, GreenBiz.com is an exceptional resource. Similar to A Fresh Green Perspective, the site provides free news articles, blogs, careers/jobs postings, event notices, newsletters, videos, and podcasts on the evolving cleantech industry. If you're considering a product or service niche in wind, solar, or anything green, this would be an ideal starting point.

For the automotive industry, an outstanding source of free information is MSNauto.com (http://autos.msn.com). From owner reviews to comparative pricing to reliability reports, the content is deep, current and surprisingly objective. Edmunds.com and jdpower.com are similarly helpful. In addition, there are hundreds of independent auto forums that discuss a range of issues from maintenance and installation of parts to lemon class action suits and fatal manufacturing flaws.

Zdnet is one of those "wow!" business technology news websites that offers a variety online portals, IT reviews, news, downloads, whitepapers and price comparisons. Zdnet is owned by CNET which caters to a different business-oriented audience with similar outstanding content. With CNET there's also TV.com, and Movie Tome; on-demand video content, with which you can take the lazy way out, sitting and watching as hundreds of hours of tutorials, guides, tips and updates are dumped into your lap.

Another superb source of pertinent free information is the U.S. government. The A-Z Index of U.S. Government Departments and Agencies (http://www.usa.gov/Agencies/Federal/All_Agencies/) is a vast information portal leading to all major government agencies including the U.S. Small Business Administration (SBA) which provides small business owners with an abundance of reports, studies, statistics, online training and regulations to assist in running a business more efficiently. The U.S. Department of Commerce with its Bureau of Economic Analysis is also a must-see government site, providing important insight into the Gross Domestic Product (GDP), corporate profits, personal income, consumer spending, travel and tourism, and international investments.

Wisdom of the Mound

Finally, and most mind-boggling in the search for reliable information sources, is the catch-all category know under the Anthead System as *Wisdom of the Mound*.

When scout ants go out from the mound to search for food, they often wander randomly throughout the forest until they find an edible food source. After consuming a portion, perhaps to authenticate its safety and at lease leverage a minimum return from the discovery, they head in a direct line back to the mound. Along the way they leave a trail of pheromones, a precise scent to lead foraging mound-mates back to the food source. As the other ants find the food and return to the mound, they also leave a scent along the trail to reinforce the original scent left by the scout.

We're on our way into deep waters again, so stay with me.

Scientists estimate there are over 12,000 different species of ants. Some species, such as the honeypot ant, raid other honeypot colonies, kill the queen, and enslave the remaining workers to help with the preservation of the original mound. The enslaved workers assist in raising the queen's offspring and even participate in locating and raiding other mounds.

These two processes offer incredible insight into the fundamentals that govern the Wisdom of the Mound.

First, look closely at the original scout ant. She is an explorer of sorts, venturing out into unknown territory, zigzagging across the hostile, sometime deadly terrain. She has no compass or map, no GPS to show her the way. She must remember the varying landmarks and points of navigation. Then, as soon as she finds food, she must carve out a new path that follows a direct line back to the mound, leaving a trail of pheromones along the way.

Once she reaches the mount, she must communicate with soldier ants that block the entrance so they will know she is part of the group and has an urgent need to get inside. Once inside, she must communicate with other foraging ants to go out and follow her trail.

There may be hundreds, even thousands of scouts out at any given time. Thus, the colony must be able to communicate which trails to follow and which food sources have been exhausted.

There are also inherent dangers associated with leaving the mound; predators such parasitic flies, natural ant-eaters and other hostile colonies competing for food. When certain areas prove to be hazardous, ants must communicate the need to avoid these areas, opting for safer terrain.

Finally, there are slave ants that formerly served as scouts and have new information about opportunities and potential dangers in foreign fields that inhabitants of the original mound may not have explored. These ants are indispensable in widening the food chain as well as solidifying the ongoing raids of other mounds.

Now what if you could drain every ounce of knowledge from every ant living in the mound and put it up on a screen or load it into a huge database? Each time an ant went out, it could check the updated findings to determine the potential food sources, predatory dangers and general unknowns. How wonderfully efficient would that be?

What I've just described is the Wisdom of the Mound. It's the totality of knowledge available in a select universe. Researchers sometimes refer to this as crowd wisdom, because it takes into account the tacit, informal, unconnected knowledge being carried around by individuals in a group or crowd.

If you've ever watched *Who Wants To Be A Millionaire*, you remember how contestants called on the audience to lend its collective knowledge to assist in answering certain questions. Similarly, open source organizations such as Firefox, Wikipedia, Joomla and MySQL rely on mass contributions by voluntary contributors to provide the critical content that keeps the company afloat.

The open source concept is based on free access and distribution of content. More importantly, it relies on the proposition that many individuals in the crowd are willing, perhaps, even eager, to share their knowledge with others in exchange for the possibility of long-term, unspecified mutual benefits for the group as a whole.

When Las Vegas bookies create a betting line on a big sporting event, the line is the results of the Wisdom of the Mount. These shrew, analytical financiers not only study the win/loss stats and historical data, but contact doctors that specialize in certain injuries and agents that know about internal disputes between players and owners, and relatives that know about ongoing player/wife domestic quarrels. One superstar quarterback threw four interceptions in a playoff game after his alleged mistress died in a private plane crash outside of Dallas a few days earlier. The bookies had this information and adjusted the line, accordingly.

According to James Surowiecki, national business contributor to *The New York Times* and the *Wall Street Journal*, crowd wisdom is most useful when it is modeled by four basic conditions:

- **independence**
- **diversity of opinion**
- **decentralization**
- **a way to aggregate the results**

Independence ... refers to an individual's prerogative to think and speak freely without fear of oppression, retaliation or ostracism by peers. If you've ever sat on a jury, you've probably had the opportunity to watch peer pressure at its best. If eleven members on the jury panel vote "yes", they quickly transform into a unified force to convince the holdout to vote with the majority. As time passes, persuasive tactics generally escalate into personal attacks and illogical reasoning. In most cases, the dissenting juror eventually gives in.

The same restriction of expression occurs in corporate boardrooms where managers fall into what social psychologist Irving Janis coined as "groupthink" compliance or consensus based on a false "team unity" mentality. There's collective rationalization and self-censorship. The idea is a bad one, but who's going to oppose it when the senior vice president says he likes it?

Wisdom of the Mound is distorted when participants are not able to contribute freely with a sense of independence without retribution. The "yes-man" complicity toward fraudulent practices is what sent Enron over the edge. If everyone in the crowd is saying "yes" because of peer pressure, the resulting information is null and void.

Diversity of opinion ... refers to the breadth and depth of differences in life experiences, core values and personality traits among participants. If the entire crowd was homeschooled in Omaha, there's a very good chance their perspective will be narrow and conservatively skewed. Their lack of interaction with a diverse universe will limit the potential accuracy of their input and make the data less applicable to the opportunities that exist in the real world.

Muhammad Ali was one of the greatest heavyweight champions of all times. But early in his career, one of the most frustrating aspects of trying to train him was his unorthodox style. With his persistent manner of dropping his head and leaning his entire body off balance while simultaneously throwing a punch, shuffling his feet and gliding to the side, trainers were tempted to pull their hair out. All the books on basic boxing fundamentals forbade this kind of behavior. Eventually, however, manager Angelo Dundee and others came to the realization his diversity of style was the key to his greatness.

Within the business crowd we refer to as corporate America, diversity can be translated into the expansion of available options to achieve organizational goals. When allowed to play out in an unbiased, unrestricted forum, a diversity of ideas appears to give certain companies such as GE and FedEx a competitive advantage. Said another way, if you were writing a boxing training manual, would you want Muhammad Ali's opinions and perspectives put in or left out?

Decentralization ... has to do with the distance between decision-makers at the top of the food chain, and those at the bottom. In a truly decentralized organization, many critical decisions are made without ever reaching the top for approval. The SDWT team concept instituted in the early 1980's by the Swedish automakers of Volvo and Saab is a prime example. Where workers once stayed at their workstations and performed repetitive tasks, they now follow the process down the assembly line, making critical decisions along the way.

It should be noted that their decisions are ultimately reviewed and even embellished by top management. But as mentioned earlier with the military strike units, many of the critical decisions are made by the boots on the ground.

Aggregator ... as the information flows in from the masses, there must be an aggregator or distiller to sift through the bits and pieces of data to determine its significance and how it can be applied to the organization's strategic goals.

At Wikipedia, a panel of researchers and editors comb through thousands of submissions to find the most accurate content about a particular subject. Sometimes competing submissions must be evaluated based on the perceived validity of the source from which it came. If President Reagan's daughter says he loved jellybeans and a top adviser says he hated them, which story will make the final cut?

Influenced by statistical analysis, Wisdom of the Mound seeks a central position on information that comes in. Statistical number crunchers understand and appreciate the moderating effect of finding the *medium, means* or *mode* of a body of data. The objective is not to go too far right or left and thereby risk falling into an abysmal sea of extremes.

Content Management Systems

There are many sophisticated content management systems that seek to collect, sort, analyze and facilitate usage of resulting knowledge streams. Over the past five years, the sale of enterprise content management software has been growing at an average rate of 35% annually. Over 60% of the nation's gross domestic product comes from the information sector, as manual processes continue to slip into oblivion.

One of the knowledge network systems receiving a great deal of publicity in recent year is a program called the Web Bot Project. Created in 1997 to predict stock market trends, Web Bot software tracks 300,000 keywords entered on the internet with an emotional context to develop a snapshot of the "collective unconscious" of the universe. This information is said to predict social and business trends, as well as certain catastrophic events 60 to 90 days in advance. The software is predicting a major worldwide catastrophe in 2012. So you should buy extra copies of this book just in case the original is burned or lost in a flood, you'll have another to fall back on.

Popular enterprise knowledge management systems, sometimes called Enterprise Resource Planning System (ERP) include:

- IBM's Global Business
- SAP Enterprise Systems (Oracle)
- Astute Solutions
- Tacit Knowledge Systems
- Absorb Learning Management Systen
- EPICOR
- AskMe Enterprise System
- Invensys Operations Management
- SAA Global, Oracle Content Management Solutions
- SYSPRO

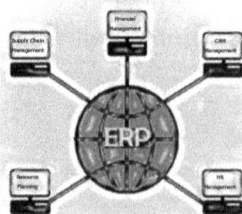

The list goes on. These systems vary in price and functionality, but essentially provide critical solutions for the discovery, mining, management and exchange of information.

Thus far, we have focused our attention on extracting information from external sources. But for a small business already up and running for a few years, there is a wealth of internal information just waiting to be discovered, organized and applied to everyday decision-making. You'll find the wisdom of your mound remarkably incomplete without the specialized insight that internal data provides.

Depending on the type of small business with which you're involved, there are six categories of knowledge you'll be working from day to day:

- **C**ustomer **knowledge** ... contacts, buying history, buying power and evolving needs.

- **C**ompetitor **knowledge** ... the strategic plans and actions taken by competitors to retain customers and gain market share.

- **P**roduct **knowledge** ... the position, price and promotional effort associated with competitive products in the marketplace.

- **P**rocess **knowledge** ... best practices, innovation in systems and technology, and synergistic opportunities for partnerships and affiliations.

- **Financial knowledge** ... the status of resources, capital and financial expertise related to a particular market.

- **People knowledge** ... tacit knowledge not formally documented, gained through experience or observation.

The key to success hinges on transforming this knowledge into reliable pillars of wisdom to support your small business operation. Don't panic. This process is not as complicated or costly as it may appear. Under the Anthead System you communicate the importance of the information, set up simple, inexpensive methods of collecting the information, process the information, and spit it out in easily discernible reports.

Before we go further, let's make some realistic assumptions, and perhaps, admit a painful truth. Optimally, what you need is an Enterprise Resource Planning System (ERP), a set of integrated software modules connected to a central database, which enables data to be shared by all departments or functionaries within the organization. But, unless you have a rich uncle or have accumulated a substantial amount of revenue in your first few years of existence, you probably won't be able to afford it. This system or a cloud computing alternative will most likely be a top priority in your 3-5 year plan.

Nevertheless, because information collection and analysis is so important to your business, you can't simply ignore it. Under the Anthead System we seek reasonable, cost effective alternatives to your eventual ERP system to ensure the collection and analysis process remains pure and your organization remains data-driven.

Having said that, as we take steps toward organizing your information system to become an intricate part of the company's daily decision-making process, you should view your choices as the best possible alternative to the ERP system you'll eventually install. These systems are falling in price each month, so you won't have to wait too long. But for now, we remain practical and take action we can afford.

Back to the installation process.

Communicating the importance of gathering and processing the information can be a deal-breaker if not handled properly. You must convey to your employees the benefits to them as well as to the long-term prosperity of the company. Otherwise, the team will rely on grapevine information that traditionally distorts the usefulness of implementation and creates a negative "more work for us" environment.

They say: Why should we take the time to input all of this research data? It's not our job.

You say: The information will make you smarter, make you operate more efficiently, make the company grow faster, open up more promotions and profit-sharing opportunities, and increase our odds of competing in the marketplace and not going out of business, thereby preventing you from having to look for another job. (Do you see how far removed that is from: *Do it because I'm your boss and I say do it?*)

Once you have buy-in from team members, the next step is to set up simple, inexpensive methods of collecting the information. Both internal and external information will be coming in from multiple sources. You'll have to break down categories of data you'd expect to receive by subject matter and software receptacles or repositories, preferably, already formatted to receive your initial input.

For instance, if the information is of a financial nature, my inclination would be to house as much as possible in Intuit's QuickBooks. That's not to say that Yodlee, Banana Accounting, YNAB, or AceMoney wouldn't do the trick. But in my experience,

QuickBooks has more functionality, is easier to navigate, has more precise reports and connects to other software database modules better than the others. Peachtree is way too complicated. And if you haven't heard, Microsoft Money had been discontinued.

Some external financial documents such as stock market analysis and annual reports will not be well suited for QuickBooks. These documents will most likely have to be scanned in and listed under a simple subheading as "Financial Reports For All Companies". You can do a search on taxonomies and tagging to develop the best classifying scheme for your data. Just remember. You're not trying to get fancy, here, but rather, rudimentary and consistent as you lay the groundwork for a future migration to a more sophisticated enterprise system.

So we scan our top competitor's annual report into a PDF file and place it into a folder on the computer. What now?

Close your eyes and imagine a Saturday afternoon just before the big game. People are streaming in from all directions, in multiple groups, wearing an assortment of clothing, and rooting for different teams. Regardless of their point of origin, diverse appearance, and team loyalties, they all end up at the ticket gate, ultimately entering the stadium and finding their designated seat in the stands. So it is with your content management system. Regardless of its source, author or relevance, all of the information ends up in a central database.

There are many different database developers ... Oracle, SQL, IBM, Sybase, and Microsoft ... to name a few. Including consulting, design, development, programming and web integration, some complex configurations can run into the millions of dollars. But because you are a startup on a strict budget or still in your years of infancy, I'm going to recommend an outstanding database with a great first name. The database is MySQL. Its first name is "*Free*".

MySQL, now owned by Oracle, is a powerful open source

relational database management system (RDBM), used by well-known companies such as Facebook and Wikipedia, to manage a diverse array of content. MySQL comes in several flavors or variations such as Drizzle, Percona Server, and transaction storage specialist MariaDB, and is scalable to meet the needs of small and large businesses alike.

To deploy in MySQL you'll need a webserver inside your office or web host using MySQL with PHP scripts already installed. You'll also need a database specialist who can customize your configuration. It would be a plus if the consultant you hire also knows Alpha Five Developer which is used to create web applications without having to know how to write code.

When hiring a database specialist, try to find someone who will agree to work for a project fee rather than on an hourly basis. It's better to incur a fixed cost rather than having to pay for the unexpected problems a developer will inevitably encounter converting database schema such as table views and integrity constraints. Let the developer know you're on a strict budget, and have him spell out in detail what he's going to do for the fee upon which you have agreed.

When the database is up and running you'll be able to input data through customized forms created by the developer. Share with him as much detailed information about your daily operation as possible. This will give him a snapshot of the functionality your organization requires.

Also ask about the availability of middleware that will convert proprietary formats coming out of QuickBooks and other software applications into compatible data for the database. QB Data Transfer - MySQL 2.0.0, for instance, is a $350 middleware that transfers QuickBooks data Exports to MySQL. Remember, the objective, even if not 100% attainable without a full-fledged Enterprise Resource Planning System, is to get all the information into one place.

Think about the many internal and external sources of information that will flow into your database. From the internet, Facebook, Twitter, business forums, newspapers and monthly business publications there will be articles, product reports, technology tips and whitepapers, government alerts, industry projections, and convention and seminar opportunities. From QuickBooks, there will be revenue and expense statements, employee timesheets, customer contact and shipping information, goods and services purchasing reports, bank account activities, federal and local income tax filings, and budget projections for current as well as future years.

If you're using a Human Resources Management System (HRMS) such as Talent Platform or Halogen Employee Performance & Talent Management Software, you'll be transferring employee salary, benefit and profile data into the MySQL database. For company projects in Excel, Access, Microsoft Project Professional, Clarizen, or IBM Rational, you'll probably need a middleware. SQLWays is the most comprehensive migration tool for MySQL; but expect to pay about $500 per license.

How do you handle the critical input of tacit knowledge, the expert one-of-a-kind experiences and observations floating around in the heads of individual employees?

You'll need to develop a knowledge network system based around an online corporate directory of expert commentary, advice, best practices and proven solutions. This network will be accessible to all employees to input or extract information as necessary.

Socialtext Workspaces (http://www.socialtext.com/) is a good example of this. The customizable wiki facilitates the circulation of information, ideas and expert advice in a targeted way with teammates, so they can collaborate freely through specific channels and activity streams, and not waste time rediscovering knowledge. Socialtext can also be set up to give customers limited access to provide input on your products and services.

One of the rewarding by-products of a knowledge network system is its ability to serve as an agent of change. We talked earlier about the impact of peer pressure on team members. Sometimes it can be used in a positive venue. When one manager learns that another manager has stopped using certain software because it's too slow, or has increased attendance in her department by offering subordinates a $100 bonus for each quarter of perfect attendance, or has switched to a vendor that's half the cost, the tendency is for the discovering manager to follow suit. Change is informal, quiet, nonresistant, and implemented from the ground, up.

Any email, posting or discussion thread from the knowledge network wiki can be copied and pasted into the MySQL database. So can email content from the regular company email system. The duplication is well worth the ultimate goal of centralizing the data for future analysis.

A deliver company might include GPS route information in the database, while a record services company specializing in legal documents might track the election of judges or the movement of lawyers from firm to firm. The possibilities are endless, depending on the business you're in.

Once the data is in one place, what happens then?

If you've ever watched the movies where an old hobo is sifting through the dump, searching for anything valuable, then you've got a pretty good idea. Your next task is to extract value from your mix-and-match compilation of information. Somewhere in that extraordinary pile of business gibberish and gobbledygook is the Wisdom of the Mound.

Media icon and billionaire Ted Turner first read a small article about the budding cable industry that eventually led him to create Cable News Network (CNN). American business magnate and co-founder of Oracle Corporation, Larry Ellison, was inspired by Edgar F. Codd's groundbreaking paper on relational database systems entitled, *A Relational Model of Data for Large Shared Data Banks*. Using $1400 of his own money he started Oracle, and is now the sixth wealthiest man in the world.

That article, paper, sales report, or random, innocuous comment by some delivery driver, joking about your main customer's frustration with a loading dock routing process is in there, inside your database, waiting to be discovered.

Perhaps, there's a complaint in there from Reed Hastings who co-founded Netflix because he didn't like the idea of being charged a late fee for returning a movie after the due date. Or maybe there's a record of the board meeting old Sam Walton of Wal-Mart had with Ben Franklin Store executives, trying to convince them they could make *more* money by selling for *less*.

It's in there. But how do we get it out?

Data Mining and Predictive Analysis

The answer begins with an intriguing process called data mining. Data mining refers to the analytical sifting of data to find new patterns, relationships, sequences and insights relative to the continued existence and growth of your business. The process is discovery-driven and multi-dimensional and tied to the realistic prospect of predicting the future.

"Do you have your Kroger Plus Card, Sir?" That's what the cashier asks each time I make a purchase at my local Kroger Food Store. Using the card generally means a few pennies off a select group of items. But for Kroger, it means a lot more. It means tracking my purchases and being able to base their business intelligence on actual profiles and transactions.

Let's say as a Kroger manager you notice a pattern. During the weekend leading up to the Fourth of July holiday, you notice some customers buy bags of charcoal along with their meat purchase of steaks, ribs and Cornish hens. By checking the purchasing history of your prime 30 - 48 year old age group, you find that your store-level observations are only partially correct. Charcoal purchases are actually declining within this group, but butane cylinder rentals are up by 35%. You were about to plan a weekend meat/charcoal promotion, but predictive analysis based on your data mining tells you that combo would be off target.

Here's another example. Let's say you're an apartment manager. In studying your rental revenue and occupancy levels, you find that 70% of the tenants that skipped out on the rent (moved out during the night with an outstanding balance) had been late in paying at least two times during the previous six months. This "sequence of events" information allows you to predict the probability that a tenant will skip based on the two late payments.

You might decide to rewrite the lease agreement requiring a larger deposit when a tenant is late two times in a six month period. This step will mitigate your losses and free up the apartment sooner, before the enviable occurs.

Under the Anthead System, the search by small businesses to find compatible niche markets is critically tied to data mining and predictive analysis. This process of placing bets on future scenarios and then deploying valuable resources to seize promising opportunities is the lifeblood of the organization's decision-making apparatus. Effectively morphing out of one opportunity and into another should not be done arbitrarily, however. You need useful information and the right tools to correctly analyze the data at hand.

Without attempting to transform you into a full-fledged research analyst, there are certain aspects of the data mining process you should understand. First, the data will fall into two separate categories. The first is primary data. The second is secondary data. Both are important, with the potential to provide pertinent information as well as flawed results.

When we look at primary information sources, we are generally talking about original market research studies or surveys that you conduct in-house or commission externally to extract specific information from a specific audience. You might want to know how your customers perceive your product's quality and durability, or whether they're satisfied with your delivery schedule. You might send out a mail survey or contact them by phone with specific questions to extract this information. This process is referred to as reactionary sampling because you're basing your ultimate conclusions on the reactions of chosen respondents.

The upside to this kind of research is its originality, customization and the overall control you maintain over the process. In certain types of focus group sessions, this reactionary approach gives you the flexibility to alter the inquiry process on the fly. For instance, if you have ten respondents in a room and nine are confused by a word or phrase used in the questionnaire, you can revise that phrase on the spot, thereby improving feedback and increasing your chances of getting the undistorted information you desire.

The down side to reactionary sampling takes us full circle to the discussion of groupthink where individuals respond based on political correctness or their perception of the groups collaborative will. Even if there is no group and the survey is conducted over the phone or online, many times respondents tend to withhold their true feelings, fearful they might offend or embarrass someone in your organization.

Many years ago one of my clients who owned three full service gas stations (Millennials are sitting there asking what does full service mean.) received a questionnaire from the Office of the Attorney General. The questionnaire was the result of many complaints state officials had received about the ongoing predatory practices of large Texas oil companies. Pursuing their strategy of vertical integration and control of all aspects of the business, several oil companies had begun to employ pricing strategies aimed at putting independents like my client out of business.

For instance, they would sell the independents wholesale gasoline three to five cents higher per gallon than the prices at their own company stores. They made independents sign exclusivity contracts to buy all tires and batteries from oil company distributors, then periodically told the independents the merchandise was out of stock, which meant when customers came in, the independents were out of stock and could not meet their needs.

It was clear their objective was to put the independents out of business. But my client was afraid to fill out the questionnaire from the Attorney General's office because lawyers for the big oil companies had forced an agreement that would allow oil company executives access to the information once it had been collected. In other words, the oil companies would be able to see which independent owners said bad things about them, and then initiate retribution further down the line. Thus, the questionnaire was useless, as it generated distorted information or no information at all.

Not all reactionary sampling is useless. In fact, if done correctly, it can be priceless in its ability to accurately reflect the true status of your universe.

Why did President Bush visit Ohio again and again during the 2004 election? Because the polls (the reactionary sampling) made it clear that the election was so tight, whoever won Ohio's twenty electoral votes would win the election. In 1985, when Coca-Cola made the soft drink blunder of the century and attempted to replace Coke with re-formulated New Coke, the public outcry along with more sophisticated reactionary sampling forced the company to bring the old Coke back.

It was not to say Coca-Cola's management had failed to do reactionary sampling prior to the decision. The company had spent four years testing the new recipe and conducting taste tests with more than 190,000 respondents. The results showed people preferred New Coke 55% of the time. But what the research failed to do was ask if respondents were willing to give up old (Classic) Coke to get New Coke. The answer would've been a resounding *No!*

In our earlier discussions, we talked about the importance of synthetical thinking, that is, how all parts work together as a whole. The Coke research did its job in identifying taste preferences. What the process failed to do was consider all the connecting pieces including our human tendency to resist imposed limitations that reduce our access to familiar choices. Creative destruction was an unacceptable consequence when it came to losing old Coke. Fast-forward twenty-five years later and we find New Coke has not only disappeared from the market completely, but the word *Classic*, used to distinguish the two, has been removed from all products.

Secondary data is different from primary data in that the research is not done by you or someone you hired. Rather, it already exists in the form of published studies, books, newspapers, trade publications and government reports. The emphasis in using this data shifts from executing reliable research techniques to choosing sources you trust.

If Donald Trump says he's going to have a real live alien on his show and the US government says there are no aliens, who do you believe?

Okay, that might be a bit too difficult to answer. But if the oil companies say we have a shortage of gasoline and Ralph Nader says there's plenty of gasoline but a conspiracy to drive prices up, who would you believe?

In using secondary research, it comes down to which source you believe has the integrity and sense of due diligence to produce accurate information. Once you've located what you feel is reliable information, then it comes down to using the proper tools to extract meaning for your organization.

There are many analytical tools capable of drilling deep into the hidden chambers of your database to extract undiscovered patterns, sequences and insights. According to Forrester Research's 2010 evaluation of predictive analytics and data mining (PA/DM) vendors, SAS Institute, IBM's SPSS and KXEN, Oracle, Portrait Software, and IBM "head the pack with mature, sophisticated, scalable, flexible, and robust solutions". SAS is the clear leader with rich features and advanced in-database analytics, while KXEN stands out for its mastering of content analytics.

The most prevalent tool used in data mining is the process called Knowledge Discovery in Databases (KDD). At the risk of overwhelming you with the complexity of the process, SAS and others embed "predictive logic" into your database to support functions such as data mining, descriptive modeling, econometrics, simulation and text analytics. The actual predictive analytics and data mining (PA/DM) tools are modules of software algorithms that attempt to identify patterns and associations in data relationships.

Stay with me here. It's not that complicated.

Think about the software that screens your email to determine which messages are legitimate and which are spam. The software uses a combination of history, source of origin, association and content to determine the probability the email is spam. If three previous emails from Joe at the Viagra store in Canada have been labeled by you as spam, and several other Canadian drug emails have been sent to your recycle bin, the software will use the history, keywords and Canada association to classify the email as spam.

Technically, this software is referred to as an intelligent agent, working repetitively in the background without human intervention. LendingTree's mortgage website uses a similar form of rule-based intelligence to qualify, or in my case, disqualify applicants for a variety of financial products.

Data mining software uses the same historical, associative, rule-based clustering approach. It looks for ways to identify key variables, relationships and anomalies as part of a pattern or association. The end results are "discoveries" that help business owners optimize their current operation and predict appropriate adjustments for the future.

Virtually all decisions are made on the information at hand. The Bush Administration invaded Iraq based on the information that Saddam Hussein was hiding weapons of mass destruction. Boston Scientific bought Guidant Corp. for $27.5 billion in 2006 based on the flawed information about its advance drug-eluting technology and the manageability of thousands of defibrillators recalls. Years later the merged company remained up to its eyeballs in debt with stock prices trading 64% below the Standard & Poor's 500 Health Care Equipment Index. Finally, revisiting a previous discussion, NASA's Jesse Moore authorized the tragic 1986 flight of Space Shuttle Challenger based on a watered-down synthetic O-rings assessment sent to him by the Morton-Thiokol's management team.

When we use contemporary terms like information systems or information management or information specialist, our minds have a tendency to skip over the critical impact that first word has on the total process. Everything starts with information. If the information is flawed or lacking, there's a very good chance the entire process will follow suit.

Information cleansing, often referred to as data cleansing, is the act of identifying, modifying and/or removing corrupt or inaccurate records from a database. Unlike data validation where the information is prevented from entering the system in the first place, data cleansing is intended to purge or correct information that has made it into the system and holds the potential to create a false read.

Let's say you're an entertainment agent managing a list of movie stars and sports figures. To show your appreciation during the holidays, you tell your secretary to send out a $5000 gold Krugerrand to all of your clients. Going through the database she sends a Krugerrand to Muhammad Ali, a Krugerrand to Cassius Clay, Jr. and a Krugerrand to the Louisville Lip. How long would it take you to realize you've rewarded the same person three times? And, are you willing to bring Smokin' Joe Frazier back from the grave to try to collect those Krugerrands back?

What if you're the main precinct judge in a tight race for city council? You tally up the votes to find Cutthroat Susie has won by ten votes. You step up to the microphone to announce the winner. A few hours later, you get a call that the voting boxes in Sleazy Jim's neighborhood were never counted. There's no way Susie could win a majority of votes in Jim's neighborhood. You already know your election results are flawed.

What I've described are the two most prevalent problems associated with data cleansing: data that's misrepresented and data that's incomplete.

How often does an inventory manager order too little or too much, based on distorted counts, misspellings, and references to the same product using a different name? Are we out of Coke, New Coke, or Coke Zero? Is factory part number XL2555 the same as XL-2555 or 2555_XL? The larger a company grows, the greater the probability that varied sources of input will represent the same data in different ways.

The other distortion has to do with data not being represented at all. You do a survey in New York City that says lawn mowers are not selling well. But you've left out Dallas, Atlanta and Birmingham where there are plenty of yards and the grass is growing year round.

The information is in your database. But because it's not "clean data", it's going to lead you astray.

Under the Anthead System, predictive analysis is imperative. You have to make bets on the future. But you must make sure the data you're analyzing represent as much of the true universe as possible. As a small business with limited historical information and a restricted budget for purchasing national research studies, the lack of representation from all segments of the total universe is probably going to be your biggest "cleansing" challenge.

How much data is enough data to declare your database to be "clean"?

The answer to this question is not simple. It depends on a number of factors including your strategic approach, the size and nature of the marketplace you serve and the number of competitors you face. The information absolutely has to address certain aspects of the marketplace to approach a sense of completeness or cleanliness. Let's take a look at the most important ones.

Competitive Forces Model Analysis

In Michael E. Porter's book *Competitive Strategy: Techniques for Analyzing Industries and Competitors,* Porter identifies five competitive forces that shape every industry and market. These forces help us to analyze everything from the strengths and weaknesses of competitors to the potential profitability of the industry.

New Market Entrants ... We talked about barriers to entry. The easier it is for new companies to enter a particular industry, the more intense the competition will be. And the greater the chances for a Netflix-type late-comer with new, improved technology to knock you off the wall.

Power of Suppliers ... If one or more suppliers (like Microsoft in the '90's) has a large enough impact to affect a company's margins and volumes, then it holds substantial power and can dictate certain terms. Google has the power right now to put many businesses out of business. Thus, if you base your entire business on creating Google applications, you should fully understand your vulnerability.

Power of Buyers ... If one or more big volume buyers (like the Air force, Navy or even Wal-Mart) have a large enough impact to affect a company's margins and volumes, then it holds substantial power and can dictate certain terms. Wal-Mart is the world's largest retailer with $245 billion in goods and services. It tells its suppliers up front "what we pay for your product must go down in price each year".

Availability of Substitutes ... Evaluating the probability that key customers will switch to a competitor's product or service? If the cost of switching is low (toothpaste), and there is little differentiation, this poses a serious threat.

Traditional Competitive Rivalry ... Evaluating the intensity of competition between existing firms in the marketplace. A highly competitive environment (Dell vs. HP) might result from a mature stage of market growth where companies can grow only by stealing customers away from other competitors. This is a formula for ongoing price wars and elevated legal confrontations in which, as a small business owner, you simply cannot afford to get involved.

As we explore the significance of traditional competitive rivalries, it is expedient to include a new anomaly that has been gradually winning acceptance in the marketplace. It is a phenomenon known as *frienemy.*

In the simplest of terms, a frienemy is a friend one day and an enemy the next day. Sounds a little like your spouse, doesn't it? Pretty close.

A classic example of a frienemy relationship would be the one between America and Russia. We love (okay, tolerate) each other one day and hate each other the next. When Russia was about to collapse, America sent billions of dollars to stabilize the economy and keep the country afloat. When America needed someone to strong arm Iran and Kosovo and negotiate with North Korea, Russia stepped in.

Russia buys billions of dollars in goods from the US and stabilizes the world oil supply which is a benefit to us. Yet, all around the globe we compete like savages.

In the business world we see frienemy relationships all the time. Considering all priorities, frienemies see only the bottom line.

Adobe makes a special version of Photoshop specifically for Apple Macintosh operating systems. And yet the two companies claw at each other's faces in the video market where Adobe promotes Premiere Pro and Apple promotes its own Final Cut Pro. The same holds true for Oracle and Hewlett-Packard. In general they are partners except when it comes to the server computer market where they fight like cats and dogs.

Imperial Sugar is on almost every grocery shelf in America. Yet, it manufactures competing sugar to go into Kroger and Safeway store brands; self labeled packages that sit on the same shelf right next to Imperial Sugar, but at a lower price. In a way, to maintain a monopolistic position in the marketplace, they are competing against themselves.

Did you know in 1997 Microsoft invested $150 million into archenemy Apple? Did you know Apple repeatedly collaborates with fierce rival Google on key desktop and mobile apps? And although Amazon has released a tablet (Kindle Fire) to compete directly against Apple, the two still collaborate on apps via the Apple Store.

What's the point? The point is shrew business operatives look for opportunities to exploit niches in the marketplace no matter if the co-exploiter is friend or foe.

Years ago, I turned down the opportunity to go after a large government contract because I refused to *get in bed with the enemy.* In hindsight, my perspective was rigid; my thinking lacked the necessary marketing sophistication to see the big picture.

As small business owners, we must view our strategic opportunities through long-range lenses. We are very capable of compartmentalizing our businesses to point where a ding on the toe doesn't make your fingers fall off. Don't operate in fear or with a small-minded, pessimistic outlook. Push ahead and take advantage of the opportunities that come your way.

Back to the original question. How much data is enough data to declare your database to be "clean"? Enough data is the amount of data it takes to address all five competitive forces. In practical terms, that means to gather research information until redundancy or duplication begins to set in.

As your business grows and capital budgets mature, you'll be able to install a formal executive support system (ESS) that assists senior executives in building models to make abstract predictions about future market conditions. For now, however, you must replicate the ESS process with your own home-grown techniques, using the resources you have at hand.

ESS gathers the data from internal and external sources, tracking key internal financial reports as well as online news sites, blogs and industry channels. There are automatic hour-by-hour feeds, flowing into the database and notifying team members based on key word priorities that reflect their individual interests. There are also company wikis that capture tacit employee knowledge through expert blogs, emails and project threads. This information also flows into the database and can be flagged by key words and subject matter to post to a specific manager's desktop.

The ESS system does all of this automatically. As the new kid on the block, however, you'll have to do it by hand. Surprisingly, the manual approach is time consuming, but not that difficult. You simply have to stay focused on the objectives you're trying to accomplish.

Home-Grown Executive Support System

First, you want your free MySQL database set up by a competent database consultant. Once you explain the particulars of your business and your emphasis on predictive analysis, he'll be able to recommend the hardware, software and middleware you'll need. Remember, you want a fee-based contract and a database consultant who knows something about using open-source software applications.

You're trying to get everything into the database. As a point of clarity, when I say database, I really mean multiple databases inside the powerful MySQL open source relational database management system (RDBM). The consultant will employ middleware (such as QB Data Transfer – MySQL) to migrate proprietary formats from other software applications such as QuickBooks and Excel into the MySQL system. He can also set up a feed from your free company wiki (Socialtext or DokuWiki) to send specific subject-related discussions into a specific database on which you can run reports and summaries. You can also subscribe to multiple websites (RSS feeds) to send alerts or even articles to your email or desktop which can then be forwarded to the database.

Now, here's the fun part. Once you've collected thirty to sixty days worth of information, it's time to dive in, head first. Your objective is to assess whether you've collected enough data to address all five areas within the competitive forces model. You can use a powerful open source (free) data mining software called Talend's Open Profiler. Or you can plow through hard copy reports, summaries, articles, emails, etc., printed from the database.

There will probably be a great deal of duplication of information. That's fine at this point, as long as the duplication is not pointing to false inventory or revenue streams. As a startup or small business in its infancy, your main concern is having a database that represents all segments of the universe.

Going through the information, you'll be able to determine whether you're ready to start making bets on the future or whether you need more data. Don't expect the process to produce an infallible crystal ball. In the final analysis, like the high-paid executives on Wall Street, you're going to be making bets or intelligent predictions on what the future will bring. The big difference now is you're not operating in isolation. Behind every decision, you have the powerful Wisdom of the Mound.

We've spent a great deal of time understanding the nature of information resources, tools and techniques. And rightly so. Under the Anthead System, the process of identifying, exploring and protecting your position in new markets will easily take up 60% of your time. You'll be making bets based on the synthetical knowledge you have of the marketplace. And, on any given day, you'll be scrambling to maximize your opportunities and minimize your risks.

Even with these amazing tools and techniques, don't expect to hit a home run each time you come up to bat. As I'm sure you have already surmised, there's a learning curve of trial and error ingrained into this process. Nevertheless, be reassured that in the long run, the time you invest in adapting to this system will pay off, handsomely.

In the next three chapters, we'll pull the entire process together under a hypothetical case study. But for now, you should feel empowered and ready to move your organization into high gear. In the *Wall Street Journal Essential Guide to Management by Alan Murray*, strategy consultant Gary Hamel was quoted as saying, "The single biggest reason companies fail is that they overinvest in what is, as opposed to what might be".

That won't be your problem. From this point forward, your entire focus will be on the extraordinary opportunities the future will surely bring.

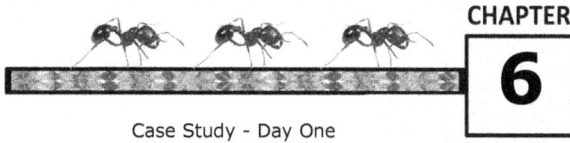

CHAPTER

6

Case Study - Day One

*W*e began this incredible journey with a hypothetical scenario that led us through a windfall of new
knowledge and innovative management techniques. What better
way to close out than with a hypothetical scenario that captures the
full essence of the Anthead Syndrome and fills our polymorphic
heads with the Wisdom of the Mound.

If you're familiar with Sydney Pollack's 1975 CIA thriller,
Three Days of the Condor, you'll remember the daily struggles
Robert Redford endured in order to survive. So it will be with
your three days inside the mound. Your objective will be to use
your specialized knowledge and skills to overcome unique business challenges typically faced by king/queen entrepreneurs, and
embrace inventive solutions that allow your company to survive
and prosper.

Here's the situation:

Background

You own Averest Plastic Enterprises, a small, four year old plastics manufacturing and distribution company in Texas. You have ten employees, all fitting the profiles designated by Anthead profile and competency recommendations. You have a modest executive office connected to a small 12,000 foot manufacturing plant/warehouse which houses several mold, die cutting, hot stamping, and silk screening machines. With the help of three highly trained technicians, you have managed to build a narrow, but reliable product line of plastic utility toolboxes, weather-resistant equipment cases, fishing tackle boxes, slim line, hinge-lock CD and DVD plastic transparent covers and bubble-lined, peel & stick mailing envelopes to serve the assorted needs of a small regional customer base.

Initially undercapitalized and struggling to stay open the first 18 months, you have watched revenues steadily climb, operations become more efficient, and customer satisfaction increase with the addition of each new product line. You currently have $600,000 in the bank and a $250,000 line of credit. Your average markup on sales is about 28%. Gradually phasing in the Anthead System over the past 8 months, you have zero employee turnover, a team with high morale, and the full expectation of doubling your business in the next two years.

At least, you had that expectation before last month.

Challenges

In the last 90 days, you've received a torrent of assorted bad news. Sales are down 40% from the previous year. A huge plastics factory has opened on the Texas-Mexico border and begun shipping plastic products into the region at half the price. One of your largest clients, Hollywood Video, responsible for over 50% of your DVD plastic cover orders, has just gone out of business. Blockbuster Video in Dallas, which gave you a small order with the promise of more to come, has filed bankruptcy. An Austin music studio that previously bought a large volume of DVD covers and plastic bubble envelops has cut back its orders because their artists are selling an increasing amount of music online as single downloads rather than hard copy DVDs.

The Texas Parks and Wildlife Department has passed a series of stringent new fishing laws reducing the number of fishermen statewide and depressing sales of fishing tackle boxes. The weather-resistant equipment cases and other commercially used equipment covers provide the greatest profit margins, and are still going strong. However, Jake Howard, your drone/enforcer, has just gotten back from a fact-finding trip to Minnesota and has informed you his finding are not encouraging. It's going to be bad news. You already know. The only question that remains is how bad.

Your three days inside the Anthead mount begin now.

Day One

Your first order of business on Monday morning is to meet with drone Howard. But before you reach your office, you find Big Mike standing in the hallway next to your office door. He needs to talk to you so you both go inside your office for an impromptu conference.

Big Mike has been a model sales manager. Accepting your inspired challenge after returning from the convention, he has mentored both Sally and Wayne, increased their call-to-sales ratios, improved their customer feedback and made them more knowledgeable about the products they sell. Overall sales, however, have continued to trend downward due to market pressures beyond their control.

Mike says: Just wanted to alert you. We're not going to make our numbers again this month.

You say: I'm aware. I know you're doing your best on your end. I'm putting together a plan to improve our position in the marketplace. Just keep plugging away as we try to get back on track.

Mike says: There's one more thing I felt I should tell you. As of this weekend, Sally and I are personally involved.

You say (laughing): Well, I did ask you to get to know her better? Of course, I didn't quite have this in mind.

Mike says: Ordinarily, I wouldn't have said anything. But you've been a straight shooter with me. I read somewhere about the legal grounds for sexual harassment. If things don't work out, I didn't want to get you or the company in trouble.

You say: I appreciate that, Mike. What I'll have to do is relieve you as manager over her. Starting today, I'll have her answer to Jake (drone Howard). That way, it can never be said you used your supervisory power to pressure her. I'll send out an official memo this morning. Meanwhile, you can still mentor, but don't supervise or give her assignments. Because you were honest with me, I'll keep your compensation the same and we'll renegotiate at the end of the year. Meanwhile, I want you to take it upon yourself to recruit another salesperson based on the Anthead criteria we've talked about. What you guys do in terms of bringing in revenue is so critical. That department is going to have to grow even more.

Note that when sales are falling, large companies generally lay off. Under the Anthead System, you're hiring. Alternatively, you're moving people into areas that show a greater potential for growth. Stated another way, you're doing everything that you can to hold on to human capital that has been molded into a unique fit for your organization.

In your meeting with drone Howard, you informed him of the proposed changes to Big Mike's supervisory status to determine if he has any objections. Verifying he is in agreement with the new arrangements, you then listen to his report.

He has just come back from touring a high tech, state of the art plastics plant in Minnesota. The multimillionaire owner of Visions Products offers a standing personal tour to anyone, including customers, competitors, community leaders, and the media to show off the upgraded facility. Unthreatened by competitor's knowledge of his operation, his objective is to gain prominence in the marketplace as an innovator and market leader.

The owner's sense of confidence stems from his superior, groundbreaking "No Molds Required" (NMR) technology which gives him a clear strategic advantage over other competitors.

Drone Howard says: The guy has purchased exclusive rights to a German fabrication technology that allows them to manufacturer plastic enclosures, housing, and panels, without using molds or tooling. We charge $800 for the RCC-1000 cover. They do the same product for $465. Some of the price points on their line of exterior covers beat us by 65% to 70%.

You say: We're already losing the low end to the Mexican plant (Quanta Plastics). Now, you're telling me it's just a matter of time before we lose the high to "No Mold" technology. What's your recommendation?

Drone Howard says: Right now, I don't have one. I just know we can't continue down this road.

The Anthead System is based on operating with speed and decisiveness. You send out an e-mail, and go around to each employee, one on one, to find out if they have special lunch plans. If not, you want everyone to complete their lunch and be in the conference room by 1:00 p.m., sharp.

At 1:00 p.m., with the exception of your delivery driver, everyone is there. You see the anxiety on their faces. Locally, Continental Airlines just laid off 60 workers; Best Buy 35; NASA, 300 and the fire department, 65. Your first order of business is to address their fears so they can focus on your visionary message.

You say: Let me reassure you this is not a mass layoff. My plan is for you and this company to be here a hundred years from now, if our wheelchairs will still get us around. I've called you together because we're a team and, under our new system, we fight adversity and share rewards together. Here's our situation.

You explain that the market is drying up and Averest has to change directions. But pursuing the wrong direction will have an adverse effect on everyone. So your plan is to collaborate with the entire team in a strategic (General Electric style) *work out* session to find the best path to success.

You say: I want you to suspend your normal activities for the rest of the day. I want you to get on the phone, call at least ten associates or relatives or job counselors you've worked with before. Find out which companies are hiring and growing, and exactly what those companies do. I want you to get on the internet, go through our central MySQL database, check your personal and company emails and wikis, maybe even talk to the pigeons in the park down the street. Look for growth sectors. Look for promising opportunities we can pursue.

If anyone wants to stay late tonight, I'll buy pizza. Maria (secretary/receptionist/data entry), I believe you told me you have relatives in El Paso. I want you to call them and find out any dirt on Quanta Plastics. I want to know what that big plant in Mexico is doing to get its prices so low. If it's child labor or under-grade materials or anything like that I'm going see if I can get the word out and get their products blackballed from the US. That will buy us some time.

Tomorrow, we'll meet again at noon. I'm having lunch brought in. The worst answer you can give me tomorrow is "I couldn't find anything."

After the meeting, Ms Daily (larvae) wants to meet with you, privately. She had scheduled a tour for the Young Business Tycoons Club at Ball Middle School three months earlier. She wants to make sure it's okay to keep the commitment.

Larvae Daily says: They're looking forward to it. I think it would really be a disappointment to them if we had to cancel. They'll be in and out in less than an hour.

You agree to keep the commitment.

Larvae Daily says: One more thing. I know you didn't mean for it to come off that way, but in the meeting it sounded as though you were already planning a smear campaign against the factory in Mexico. You seemed to be encouraging Maria to give you a starting point.

You say: It's my job to protect this company any way I can. That's how we keep eating and paying the mortgage.

Larvae Daily says: Not "any way", at least that's not what our mission states. There's a whole section in our policies manual that talks about ethical business practices and a commitment to the "high road" of social consciousness. There's nothing there about bad-mouthing the competition, or dirty tricks to get ahead. You are our leader. When people see what you do, they figure it's okay to do it too.

You say: Ms Daily, don't you have something better to do, like visiting the federal prisons and lecturing some of the Enron executives?

She smiles, then leaves, knowing you've heard her appeal

to stay true to your company's core values. To maintain trust and credibility, managers must not just talk the talk, but walk the walk as well. So much for your brilliant smear campaign.

You devote that afternoon to searching your MySQL database for trends associated with promising niche markets. Your free DokuWiki and Talend Open Studio provide a steady flow of customer and employee observations that give insight into unmet needs and foreseeable changes in the marketplace. An article on the automobile industry's switch to fuel efficient hybrid and electric engines catches your attention. Due to The National Highway Traffic Safety Administration (NHTSA) and US Environmental Protection Agency's (EPA) mandate to transition to lighter vehicles that produce more fuel efficiency, many of the assembly parts for new vehicles will be made of plastic. Even more encouraging is the federal government's plan to spend a minimum of 15% of the billions in subsidies with small, women and minority businesses. That would mean "locked in" revenue for which the larger corporations couldn't compete.

You discover there are new hybrid factories opening up in Dallas, Oklahoma City and Little Rock. Your proximity to these locations gives you a strategic advantage in lower shipping costs and face-to-face customer service. The more you read about the subject, the more you're convinced this growing niche is right for you.

You walked out to the plant/warehouse to speak directly with the technicians to get their expert perspective on transitioning to plastic parts for light weight vehicles. So the product line will continue to flow, you discover the three techs are alternating between working the machines, making calls and researching market opportunities on the computer. You congratulate them for finding a way to satisfy your immediate research request as well as addressing the ongoing production needs of the company. This is the kind of team collaboration you've instilled under the Anthead System, with many operational decisions being made by the tech team and never having to reach top management for approval.

You want to speak with all three techs. But one is across the street at the service station.

Tech One says: Riley had to use the restroom. He'll be right back.

You say: Why is he going across the street to the gas station to use the restroom? We have a restroom here in the work area, and two in the front office.

Tech Two says: Yeah but Riley is 6ft 4 in, 350 pounds. Those toilets are too small for him.

You say: Okay, tell him I'll be back in half an hour.

In the hallway you run into drone Howard.

You say: Did you know Riley is going across the street every day to use the restroom?

Drone Howard says: Yes. Our facilities are too small. I priced the parts and labor for an upgrade in the warehouse restroom and it was just too high, almost $900. That was five months ago. Prices have probably gone up by now.

You say: Once we get this market search behind us, I'd like for you to look into it again. Sending an employee across the street doesn't feel right.

That afternoon, as you continue your quest for a suitable marketing niche, your mind keeps drifting back to Riley's situation. Would Southwest Airlines or Ben & Jerry's have their employees go across the street to use the restroom? Certainly your commitment to your employees is no less passionate.

You go online to see if there is any information on larger toilets. With a strategic crisis looming, allocating precious time to toilet-hunting doesn't feel rational. However, your founding commitment to value each person in your organization, putting both customers and employees first, overrides your instincts to use common sense.

The information you find is astounding. The market is about to explode.

Though, Japanese toilet makers have historically dominated the world of bathroom innovation with their posterior shower jets, odor-deterring perfume bursts, noise-masking audio effects and quiet-flush technology, an aging population and global scarcity of water has ushered in a new generation of toilets for health-conscious, comfort-oriented, conservation-minded consumers. There are larger, heavy-duty models for an increasingly obese population, intelligent models for aging Baby Boomers to monitor weight, blood pressure and urine samples, men models with automated lifting lids, and water-efficient model requiring only 1.6 gallons per flush, as opposed to the older toilets requiring 5 gallons per flush.

What's more, besides a few established names in the marketplace such as Daiwa House, Kohler and Toto, there are no dominate players in the new arena of toilet transformation, with newer models in final testing stages, approaching initial distribution. For all practical purposes, the market is still wide open.

You call a local toilet distributor. The Toto heavy-duty, extra elongated model is running about $500. Because the product is relatively new and not yet in demand, the distributor has only one in stock. You order the toilet and pay an extra $75 for same day delivery. Even if the market niche turns out to be a useless rabbit trail, you still have a commitment to address Riley's special needs.

Later that afternoon, returning to your manufacturing plant

to discuss the possible transition to plastic automobile parts, you also want to explore the potential for entering the toilet market. But there's a problem. If you engage in an extended conversation about toilets, everyone's going to be looking at a Riley. Any future activity will be associated with his many trips across the street.

Showing sensitivity within an organization is not always natural or intuitive. For this reason, since its early introduction by industrial psychologist Kurt Lewin back in the late 1940's, corporate sensitivity training has become a big business. Sensitivity training addresses concerns such as gender sensitivity, multicultural sensitivity, and sensitivity toward those who are disabled. Its objective is to educate employees in a way that alters adverse core beliefs and transforms attitudes so that an individual or individuals engage in more constructive behavior.

Back in 2006, Chicago White Sox manager Ozzie Guillen was fined an undisclosed amount of money and ordered to undergo sensitivity training for his derogatory sexual orientation slurs against Chicago Sun-Times columnist Jay Mariotti. In 2010, former Tea Party Express Chairman Mark Williams agreed to undergo sensitivity training for the infamous "Colored People" letter to President Lincoln, posted on his blog.

The headlines might lead you to believe sensitivity training is needed only for those who engage in offensive public tirades or take embarrassing missteps that insult specific groups. On the contrary, sensitivity training is actually needed for all participants on the frontline of diversity, from families with strict, generationally entrenched fathers, battling it out with rebellious, new-age children, to high-level ambassadors visiting dignitaries in foreign lands. If we have different backgrounds, personal experiences and core values, there is a high probability we're going to step on each, other's toes. How do we minimize those steps and mitigate the ensuing pain?

In an article based on her book, *The Leader as a Mensch: Become the Kind of Person Others Want to Follow,* Bruna Martinuzzi reminds us:

"We need to use our reasoning ability to understand another person's thoughts, feelings, reactions, concerns, motives; This means truly making an effort to stop and think for a moment about the other person's perspective in order to begin to understand where they are coming from: And then we need the emotional capacity to care for that person's concern...."

In this instance, without formal training, you have embraced a "common sense" approach that exceptional leaders must possess. It's not to say you won't stumble in the future. Rather, it's to say a general sense of empathy and concern for your employees' perspective will, in most instances, build positive relationships and keep you out trouble.

You decide to reserve the introduction of the toilet manufacturing and distribution option until the luncheon scheduled for the following day.

That same afternoon, drone Howard walks into your office.

Drone Howard says: I just finished another bellyaching session with Sharon Prewett (soldier/accountants). At this point, I'm about ready to show her the door.

You say: What's the problem?

Drone Howard says: She says the problem is balancing all the financial stuff with your request to do research. But the real problem is her unhappiness with the new system. She's had a barrel of complaints since we implemented the system months ago. She doesn't seem able to adjust, and her comments to other team members are not helpful. She's really become a pain in the rear.

You say: I understand how you feel. But it's always better to have an employee comfortable expressing herself than operate in silent frustration. Think about it this way. Which is the best customer to have? One that walks in the door and says, "Hey, every time I come in here it takes forever to get someone to help me." Or the customer that walks in, stands at the counter a few minutes and then leaves?

Drone Howard says: The loudmouth, I guess.

You say: You bet. Because, with the vocal customer, you have a chance to correct the problem. But with the silent customer, it's loss business. That customer is never coming back again.

Drone Howard says: That's not a fear factor. I don't think I'd lose sleep if she left and never came back again. But I do understand what you're saying about maintaining an environment based on open exchange. You have an intervention in your back pocket for a loudmouth?

You say: Not really. If she can't adjust to the Anthead System, the only intervention would be to find her a more traditional organization to work. Ask her to stop by my office when she gets a chance.

Drone Howard is a left brain (analytical/sequential) thinker. Because of his no-nonsense, linear approach to getting things done, it is critical that you, the king/queen, devote sufficient time mentoring him about the long term consequences of suppressing dissenting views. Perhaps, if enough people had dissented at Tyco or WorldCom, the circumstances for those companies would've been different.

Before soldier/accountant Prewett makes her way to your office, another problem arises. Secretary/receptionist Maria walks into your office with the product delivery report you had requested several days earlier.

After handing you the report, she stands there a few seconds.

Secretary/receptionist Maria says: I called my older brother and aunt in El Paso. They don't know much about Quanta Plastics except it's rumored the foreman that gives you the job takes part of your check every week as a payoff. Will that kind of information help you?

You say: Actually, Ms Daily has brought some new information to my attention. So I don't think we'll need to publicize what Quanta does.

Still standing in front of your desk, a bit nervous:

Secretary/receptionist Maria says: What do you think about Anti-aging cosmetics? Would that be a bad idea for our company to start selling products like that?

You immediately recognize the source of her apprehension. Maria has completed one year of community college with no direct business experience. Your request that she "morph" into an expert researcher and business planner has her afraid she will come off looking dumb and incompetent at the meeting. Her hope is to get your blessing of her idea before she presents it to the entire group.

For the king/queen entrepreneur, this is a special moment. You have the opportunity to cultivate a small seed, enabling it to blossom into what could one day become a beautiful flower.

How often have you witnessed a parent strip a child of hope and confidence with a response like "that's the stupidest thing I've ever heard" or "what's wrong with you? Do you ever think before things come out of your mouth?" The child is devastated, and sometimes, never tries again. His or her potential greatness is lost in the blink of an eye.

So it is in business when employees present new ideas.

In his article, "*How Do I Encourage Employees to Submit Ideas*", business-communication consultant Jason Gillikin states: *Some ideas might be politically risky. Make sure employees realize that they can submit ideas that might cross the "party line", and that they will be free from the threat of retribution (or embarrassment) for doing so. This commitment needs to come from the owner or president.*

You say: Wow! I can tell you've been doing your homework. The aging population of Baby Boomers still has a great influence on this country. I was reading somewhere that by 2020, 60 million North Americans will be 65 years of age and older.

Secretary/receptionist Maria says: Yes, and they're all into this fitness, wellness, and being young again. My sister is selling a line of cosmetics that restores the skin to its youthful beauty. She goes from one house party to the next. And she's doing great!

You say: Good work, Maria. This Baby Boomer angle might have some potential. As you continue to research, just make sure it's something that fits us as a company. We have a manufacturing plant next door, so let's see if we can use it in the plan.

Secretary/receptionist Maria says: You mean, like making our own cosmetics?

You say: Maybe. I'll leave it up to you to find out more about how the stuff is actually made. Will we have to buy some expensive secret oils from the Orient, or can we throw some chickens in a pot out there in the warehouse and sell the juices as reinvigorating nourishment from the Texas Hill Country?

She's laughing as she leaves the office; reassured her efforts are legitimate and potentially impactive to the team. Often referred to as The Pygmalion Effect, as a respected leader, you have the potential to have a positive impact on the rest of her career.

Secretary/receptionist Maria says: I'm going to check on those chickens right now.

You take a deep, reflective breath, never minimizing her potential to grow. Two years earlier, you had no idea what data mining or predictive analysis or morphing to new niches meant. Now you're leading the hunt. Ralph Nader once said, "I start with the premise that the function of leadership is to produce more leaders, not more followers." For all you know, you may be grooming the next CEO of your company.

Finally, you refocus your attention on the delivery report.

Many of your plastic products are delivered directly to local retailers and distributors by the company cargo van and two pickup trucks. With the new GPS system installed on each vehicle, you're able to identify stops at specific customer locations, time between deliveries, mapping efficiency and costs in driver hours associated with the delivery of each order.

According to GPS reports from the previous month, your driver, Manuel Ortega, has been making unauthorized stops. Although you've received only one customer complaint about a late delivery, you want to be proactive and not allow the situation to get out of hand.

The GPS summaries from the prior two weeks indicate driver Ortega has increased his unauthorized stops. You realize something must be done.

You walk out to the loading dock where he's packaging products for a large order headed to Austin, Texas.

You say: Hello Manuel. How's everything going?

Driver Ortega says: Fine. But busy. I keep very busy.

You say: Yes, I noticed you weren't at the meeting yesterday. I saw where you had to make an emergency delivery downtown.

Driver Ortega says: Yes. Customer called at the last minute. But they are a big customer to us. I had to go.

You say: That's one thing I can say about you, Manuel. No matter what the situation is, we can always count on you. Do you remember when you drove through the floodwaters after the hurricane to get those emergency plastic food covers to the Red Cross location? I still tell people about the courage and discipline you showed during that crisis.

Driver Ortega says: It was kind of scary. But we had to get it done, right?

You say: Scary is putting it mildly. With all those deep ditches and downed power lines, it must've been quite nerve-racking. Plus, we had that old Utilimaster Step Van I bought from the auction. It really didn't need flood waters as an excuse to stall out on you.

Driver Ortega says (laughing): Yes, we called it the smoking ghost because sometime you driving it and the power just disappear. But this new Freightliner is much better, more power and more room.

You say: You know what I like most about this new Freightliner van is the satellite-based Global Positioning System (GPS). You're familiar with GPS aren't you?

Driver Ortega says (frowning): Sort of....

You say: With GPS installed in the van and the trucks, I can pinpoint every place our vehicles go, how long they stay there and how much in man-hours each delivery costs. (You allow him to glance at the report.)

Driver Ortega says (with growing anxiety): Every place?

You say: Yes, every single stop. That way I can budget for fuel, man-hours and other shipping costs that go along with certain kinds of deliveries. It works for me and for you because it keeps me abreast of how much it's costing the company to have a dependable in-house driver like you, rather than contracting the deliveries to outside hotshot delivery services. I know I can trust you to do the right thing by our products and our company. So I don't plan to change a thing. I've got to go now. Like you, I'm very busy too. But you be careful and drive safely on your trip to Austin.

In the old days, under the Traditionalist command structure, you would've stormed out to the loading dock, chewed him out for goofing off on company time, and threatened to fire him if he ever did it again. In essence, you would've taken away his dignity and created a counterproductive, confrontational relationship between you and him. Under the Anthead System, you employ a more sophisticated, multi-tiered approach using a combination of guilt, ambiguity and future consequences to resolve the issue.

Driver Ortega feels guilty because he has violated the trust you've placed in him. He is also uneasy because, in your ambiguous discussion, he doesn't know if you are aware of his violations. Finally, with outside hotshot contractors as a realistic alternative, he realizes a continuation of his behavior will result in unwanted consequences, most likely, losing his job.

Also, with the use of Appreciative Inquiry, you have gently

nudged him into the Dream phase of the four-D model: Discovery, Dream, Design, and Destiny. You have encouraged him to envision himself as if the high performance moments of his career are the rule, perpetually practiced at all times, rather than the exception.

The beauty of this approach is that the ultimate decision remains in his hands. It is "his" prerogative or "his" choice to stop his negative behavior. His manhood is still intact. Next month's GPS reports will tell you whether he has the self-discipline to reel in his excesses or whether he will have to be replaced.

Back at your office, soldier/accountant Sharon Prewett is waiting.

> **Soldier/accountant Prewett says:** I knew it would only be a matter of time before he came and told you.
>
> **You say:** Told me what?
>
> **Soldier/accountant Prewett says:** That I won't pay his expense reimbursement.

Through continued conversation, you learn soldier/accountant Prewett is holding up expense reimbursement checks for scout/salesman Wayne. Company policy requires all sales personnel to turn in a monthly sales expense sheet, even if they don't incur expenses during that month. After repeatedly asking scout/salespersons Sally and Wayne to turn in their missing expense sheets from previous months, Sally has responded. But Wayne has not. Soldier/accountant Prewett has informed Wayne she will not issue any more reimbursement checks on current expenses until he brings his vouchers up to date.

> **You say:** Actually, I was not aware of the situation. But now that we're discussing it, what is their reluctance about turning in their reports and getting paid?

Soldier/accountant Prewett says: Mostly, because salespeople hate paperwork. But there is also the possibility of a discrepancy between the sales activity report and the expense report. If they say they've called on a certain client and took the client to lunch, why wouldn't there be an expense reimbursement request for that lunch? After two or three month's it's too foggy in their mind to regurgitate what they really did. So they don't want to turn anything in.

You say: You think the salespeople are falsifying the reports?

Soldier/accountant Prewett says: Not the expense reports, because they have to turn in receipts with each request. But the daily activity reports are a different story. I just think that sometimes they put stuff down so Big Mike will see they're busy. He pushes them pretty hard, you know.

You say: What is your recommendation to solve the problem?

Soldier/accountant Prewett says: Oh, I've solved the problem. Once they see their money is being held up, they respond. Wayne will have his two missing reports in by Friday.

You say: Thanks, Susan, for rectifying the situation. I will also have Jake and Big Mike talk to them about the importance of accuracy of their reports.

Soldier/accountant Prewett says: So if it's not Wayne's reimbursement checks, what do you need to talk to me about?

You say: I know you're not happy with the new system. I wanted to see if there were any aspects of our procedures that we could change to make things more accommodating to you.

Soldier/accountant Prewett says: Honestly, I don't think so. I just don't like the idea of being stretched all over the place. I guess I'm kind of old-fashioned, you know, believing you do what you were hired to do. This new system seems to want a lot more. It's really hard getting used to it.

You say: It was an adjustment for me too, relinquishing power, justifying my decisions to my own employees, staying true to certain values that tie my hands. But I've adjusted and I can already see the dividends.

Soldier/accountant Prewett says: Frankly, I don't think I can adjust. I didn't want to quit and leave you out on a limb. But this may be a good time to discuss my leaving the company.

You say: I hate to see you go. But I believe you deserve to be happy in your work environment. If there's anything I can do as far as recommendations, making personal calls to other owners, or even paying your headhunter expenses if it comes down to that, you can rest assured I will.

Soldier/accountant Prewett says: I know you will. Since I've been here, you've been very fair to me. Why don't we plan for me to officially leave in thirty days? That'll give you ample time to find a replacement. I'll submit my resignation letter and keep you informed of my transition into another opportunity. Who know? I might even start my own company.

She gives you a big hug and exits the office.

This is your first casualty since embracing the Anthead System. Not everyone is suited for its ambiguous dynamics and ever-evolving structure. This is a reality you will have to accept.

In recent years, over-zealous personnel managers have adopted a harsh and often unnecessary "cardboard box" policy where they pack up an employee's personal belongings in a cardboard box and have the security guard escort them to the gate. Fearful of being sued if the policy is not uniformly applied to all employees on an indiscriminate basis, they march troublesome, as well as loyal, respected, non-confrontational employees out exactly the same way.

Under the Anthead System, the "cardboard box" tactic should seldom, if ever, have to be used. Like GE or Google, most people don't want to leave. If they do, because you've treated them so well, their exit will be one of mutual respect and absent of any drama. If they're not performing, they will have been fully advised of their shortcomings with ample time and support to either improve or find a more suitable work environment.

Of course, there are always bad apples and unique exceptions to every rule. So, for the sake of company security, the "cardboard box" policy should not be totally abandoned. Just know each time you have to use it, there's a strong implication of an inadequacy in the hiring, training, mentoring or placement process.

Finally, before the day is out, you must respond to an oversight in your workout process. Secretary/receptionist Maria has brought to your attention her unspoken reluctance to present her research finding to the entire group. How many more employees, unaccustomed to the new procedure, feel the same way?

You send an email out, as well as visit each individual employee to give them an alternative to the verbal "open discussion" presentation.

> **You say:** If you're more comfortable writing out a minimum two page summary of your recommendations and leaving them anonymously in the suggestion box until it makes the final cut, you may do so. But if it is chosen, be prepared to elaborate and take full ownership.

With this embellishment, the stage is set. You still have some additional research to do. But for all practical purposes, your day is done.

Case Study - Day Two

Day Two

*A*t the noon luncheon in the main conference room, you are pleasantly surprised to walk into an electrically charged atmosphere, buzzing with anticipation. Everyone is present, the manufacturing plant is locked down and two temps are manning the telephones. Drone Howard has instructed high-tech worker Bradford Hines to set up the conference with a couple of research computers, erasable boards and a laptop projector for your presentation.

You allow some time for them to enjoy their box lunches and socialize as a group. This is an excellent opportunity to promote unity and collaboration across invisible departmental fences and foster a sense of organizational camaraderie for the journey ahead.

185

Finally, you begin.

You say: I wanted to thank all of you for breaking away from your normal routines to come together and contribute to this critical process. I use the word *critical* because what we do in this room will have a monumental effect on all of us. So many companies have gone down the tubes for not being able to adjust, or for making the adjustment in the wrong direction. We don't want that to happen. And, we're pretty confident, with the great minds sitting in this room, that won't happen.

All of you have been diligently researching the opportunities and possibilities available for a new direction. I've already heard a few promising ideas and I'm sure there are many more. What we need to keep in mind is that this process is based on collaboration, not criticism. Somewhere in our collective consciousness, our unique experiences and our exposure to different aspects of society lay the best solution to the challenge we face. But this solution will never surface if we spend our time beating each other down.

So let me conclude this introduction by saying there are no bad answers. There are no useless contributions. The smallest fiber of insight can lead to a brilliant solution. Don't hold back and don't hold anyone else back.

With the stage set, you plow into the thick of it. You develop a loosely constructed framework anchored in SWOT analysis to keep everyone on track. This is relatively simple. SWOT analysis is a strategic planning method that evaluates the Strengths, Weaknesses, Opportunities, and Threats involved in a business venture.

- **Strengths** ... characteristics of the business or team that give it an advantage over others in the industry.

- **Weaknesses** ... characteristics that place the firm at a disadvantage relative to others.

- **Opportunities** ... external chances to make greater sales or profits in the environment.

- **Threats** ... external elements in the environment that could cause trouble for the business.

Now that you've gotten everyone to think in terms of adaptable strategies, you ask if anyone would like to volunteer to be first.

It doesn't surprise you that your high-tech worker, Bradford Hines, volunteers to go first. The red-haired, thirtyish, tech-savvy network administrator represents the quintessence of your effort to (on your limited budget) hire the best and the brightest. With his enormous energy and thirst for new challenges, the workout session presents an unanticipated opportunity to keep him engaged.

High-tech worker Bradford says: I have two recommendations. The first is cloud computing which is new to the marketplace and growing at an estimated 30% annually. Most recent surveys show this will be a high growth sector for the next three to five years.

In general terms, cloud computing is any sold-on-demand subscription-based or pay-per-use internet service that increases storage capacity and/or access to software applications without investing in new infrastructure, training or software licensing. These services fall into three categories: Infrastructure-Services, Platform-Services and Software-Services. Users need nothing more than a personal computer and internet access to take advance of these services.

Your objective is to get all of the options out on the table before evaluating the merits of each. You write cloud computing on the board for everyone to see.

You say: You're getting us off to a great start, Bradford. What is your second recommendation?

High-tech worker Bradford says: My second recommendation is home security apps for the Android, iPhone and Blackberry Smartphone market. Apple alone shipped 48 million iPhones in 2010, and the number of phones using the Android system is already up to 23 million. Combine that with the fact that only about 20% of residential homes have an alarm system, and with people moving back to the city, concerns over crime and break-ins are growing. So really, it's two growth markets in one.

You write home security apps for Smartphones on the board.

You say: Sounds like you've really done your homework, Bradford. I appreciate that. We'll get our entire list together and then we'll go through to see which options best fit our company. Now who would like to be next?

Scout/salesperson Sally raises her hand.

Scout/salesperson Sally says: I have an idea, maybe not as promising as what Bradford is talking about.

You say: We'll get a chance to place a value on everything later. Right now, I'm eager to hear about your idea.

Great leaders facilitate, empower and encourage every step of the way. You reassure her that her contribution is valuable.

Scout/salesperson Sally says: I've been looking into parent outsourcing. As you know, I'm a divorced mother with a teenage son that's only a year from graduation. He wants to go to college but his grades aren't that good. He has to do well on the SAT and ACT, pass two state certification tests to graduate, and then a college entrance exam. I had to do a lot of research on test preparation services, professional tutoring services and psychological screening. It's a $50 billion dollar industry and the fees are huge. I figure with so many working parents too busy to deal with these issues, a consolidated one-stop service should be very successful.

You add it to the list.

You say: Sounds very promising, Sally. Wish this kind of help would've been around when I graduated.

If you're familiar with the term "holding a poker face", you already understand what I'm about to say. Despite your initial

189

reservations about the options being presented, you must make it a point to avoid any show of favoritism or predisposition toward an idea, even if it seems far-fetched or misaligned in terms of your organizational competencies. Remember, this is a new experience. Team members are hanging on your every word and expression. The slightest negativity on your part will drive potentially good ideas back into the ground.

You say: Okay, who's next?

Three or four hands go up at once.

This is the moment for which you've been waiting. The team's eagerness to participate means you have successfully navigated through the initial pitfalls of doubt, fear and cynicism, to reach a new phase of collective "buying in". At this juncture, the group actually believes the process is worthwhile or at least has a legitimate chance of delivering on your stated goals. Without saying it, or perhaps, consciously realizing it, team members have wadded into a pool of ambiguity with little structure and no guaranteed outcome. Under the Anthead System, this is precisely what you want; team members not afraid to leave their comfort zone, willing to manage ambiguities, and eager to tackle problems they've never faced before.

This development of precious human capital at the ground level is the single most important component in establishing your organization's strategic advantage over other competitors. This is what GE and Cisco Systems and Google do. They unleash the enormous energy, innovations and collective wisdom in their "mounds" to pinpoint root causes of problems, and hidden opportunities that will foster continued growth and profitability.

Three hours into the workout session you have ten options

on the board. Here is the list of contributors and recommendations:

High-tech worker Bradford

OPTION #1

Cloud Computing: Any sold-on-demand subscription-based or pay-per-use internet service that increases storage capacity and/or access to software applications without investing in new infrastructure, training or software licensing.

OPTION #2

Home Security Apps: For the Android, iPhone and Blackberry Smartphone market.

Scout/salesperson Sally

OPTION #3

Parent Outsourcing: Test preparation services, professional and specialized tutoring services, mentoring and psychological screening services.

Secretary/receptionist Maria

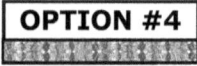

OPTION #4

Aging Products: Development and distribution of an assortment of cosmetics, organic and energy supplements aimed at the aging Baby Boomer market.

Scout/salesperson Wayne

OPTION #5

Diamond Tools Sales and Distribution: Sale and distribution of high wear resistance diamond blades, core bits, cup wheels, router bits and grinders to accommodate the massive hundred-billion-dollar construction explosion, planned for America's infrastructure.

Delivery driver Ortega

OPTION #6

Green Haul and Clean up: With so many petrochemical plants, ship channel businesses and oil companies in the area, there continues to be a shortage of certified clean-up, soil testing and spill prevention companies.

Drone Howard

OPTION #7

Prisoner Transport: Using new state-of-the-art natural gas trucks to cut fuel costs in half, the company would address the growing prison population overcrowding issue, transporting prisoners in and out of state to underutilized facilities.

Scout/sales manager Big Mike

OPTION #8

Electric Batteries for Hybrid Vehicles: Energy-efficient batteries for the upcoming line of government mandated electric cars.

Manufacturing plant workers (3) – Joint recommendation

OPTION #9

Energy Conservation Sales and Service: Servicing a growing retail market of energy-efficient minded consumers wanting to cut down on home heating and cooling costs using solar, wind and biofuel alternatives.

Larvae Daily

OPTION #11

In-Home Senior Care: Contracted healthcare assistance for the aging Baby Boomer market.

This is a big deal. Somewhere on the board is a shining window to your uncharted future. You'd like to stick your head ... no ... whole body through that window right now. But you sense the group's mental fatigue and suspect this is a good stopping point until tomorrow's session.

You say: You've done a wonderful job thus far. I'm so proud to have you on this team. Why don't we stop here and plan to resume tomorrow with our sights set on choosing the option or options best suited for the future of this company? Everyone okay with that?

There's silence in the room. Everyone's staring at you. Finally, Secretary/receptionist Maria reveals the source of their anxiety.

Secretary/receptionist Maria says: You haven't told us about your suggestion.

High-tech worker Bradford says: Yes, what did your research turn up?

As the leader of the team, you have called for an urgent, companywide action to be taken. You have instructed everyone on the team to essentially drop what they were doing and morph into research analysts, scouring the earth for promising opportunities that will keep the company afloat. Everyone on the team (with the exception of Soldier/accountant Prewett who is leaving the company) has complied. That is, everyone but you.

Are you above the law? Are you one of those leaders who orders his troops to "do as I say, not as I do"?

In earlier chapters we talked about the steps you must take to win your team's trust. These are Xers and Millennials. They watch your actions and reactions at each fork in the road to see if you're going to do what you said you would. This is a huge fork. They want to know if you're a "sleazy shuffler", or if the call to battle applies to you too.

There's another reason they're eager to examine your option. They want to compare the soundness or validity of their recommendation to yours. If legendary Lakers coach Phil Jackson asked you to prepare a game plan against the Boston Celtics, and said he would do the same, at the end of the day, you'd want to know all of the elements included in his plan and how closely your plan mirrored his. As the leader and coach of the Averest Plastic Enterprises team, your team members have taken for granted you know more about the process than they do. In essence, you are their expert. They want to know how their decision-making process stacks up against yours.

This request pushes an old dilemma to the forefront. Your primary recommendation is the development and distribution of sophisticated energy-efficient toilets. You also have the production of plastic assembly parts for EPA- mandated lighter vehicles as a promising backup. But 6 ft 4 in, 350-pound plastics technician Riley is sitting right there in the conference room. If you start to talk about toilets, there is the probability you'll create an uncomfortable situation for him.

For now, the plastic assembly parts will have to suffice.

You say: I've been looking at a new market created by the Environmental Protection Agency mandating the use of light plastic assembly parts in new fuel-efficient vehicles. Since we're in the plastics business, it might not be such a difficult transition to adapt our equipment and business model to take advance of the opportunity.

But I'm not sold on it. I'm still looking at a couple of options that might turn out to be more promising. And with the recommendations you guys have presented, we'll just have to work the process to see which options rise to the top.

High-tech worker Bradford says: Exactly, how do you plan to work the process? Is there a formula besides this SWOT analysis?

You say: Yes, it's called AUME which stands for Anthead Universal Method of Elimination. It's a bit too complicated to get into the process today. But believe me, before tomorrow is over, you all will be experts at it.

As team members exit the conference room, you take a deep breath and then slowly exhale. The meeting has been a success. But there is still one thing you need to do.

You catch technician Riley before he leaves and ask him to take a walk with you. You accompany him to the back of the warehouse and show him the new toilet that has recently been delivered.

You say: I owe you an apology. I didn't realize you had been going over the gas station across the street. It might take us a few weeks to get this installed. But I wanted to let you know how important it is for you and all other team members to be comfortable with the working environment.

Technician Riley says: No problem. You do what you have to do. The good thing is I'm losing weight and coming off this medication in a month or so. That should cut down on the trips.

You say: That's good to hear. Actually, this whole thing might end up working to our benefit. While pricing the different models, I discovered a very promising market in high-tech toilet development and distribution. These things are larger, more energy-efficient, and loaded with bells and whistles. I want to learn more about them, however, before I present the idea to the group.

Technician Riley says: When you said larger, you had my attention all the way. Let's hope this market works out for us. I might be your first customer.

There! That's it. You've dotted all "I's" and crossed all "T's". Pull out your Blackberry and file this day in the mound as a glowing success. Now it's time to go home, get a good night's sleep and prepare for the grand finale. See you tomorrow.

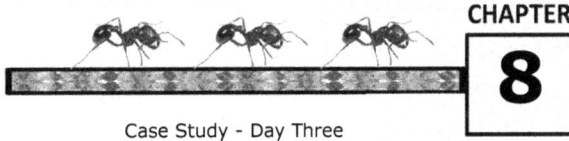

CHAPTER

8

Case Study - Day Three

Day Three

*A*s you drive into the company parking lot and slip into your Anthead gear, there's a serious conversation you need to have with yourself. It has to do with yesterday's resounding success and today's potential disaster. In management, it's sometimes referred to as "manipulated confidence" and the flawed decision-making that generally flows out of it. Though the effect is not limited to business, it is most prevalent when difficult team decisions take place.

Before General George Custer's disastrous last stand at Little Big Horn, he was admired as a fearless Union commander who fought alongside his soldiers with reckless abandon and flamboyant confidence. He made a name for himself at the battle of Gettysburg and the battle of the Shenandoah, and led very successful campaigns against the Cheyenne Indians. Then, he and his officers made a reckless miscalculation at the battle of Little Big Horn and ended up getting the tops of their heads cut off.

In 1999 Pets.com stormed onto the internet with aggressive discount pricing, free shipping, a standout Super Bowl ad, an appearance in the Macy's Thanksgiving Day Parade and a company sock puppet mascot that appeared on *Good Morning America*. With a "Can Do" attitude, funding from Amazon.com and oversight by respected venture capital firm Hummer Winblad, what could possibly go wrong? In a word: *everything*. Three hundred days and $300 million dollars later, the company was out of business.

In more recent years, Microsoft was forced to pull the plug on its Kin Smartphone less than two months after it hit the market. Microsoft, the big brother of success with decades of victories under its belt, jumped into a volatile, fast-paced, social media-oriented market in which it was not fully prepared to compete. All the money it spent buying Sidekick maker, Danger, as well as the millions of dollars promoting the new product went quietly down the drain.

What's the point?

The point has to do with your complex role as a leader. You must strike a delicate balance between encouraging your troops to be confident, fearless risk-takers while avoiding a false sense of invincibility. Financial institutions have a shrewd way of putting it: *"Past performance does not guarantee future results."* In other words, just because we made you money on your investment in the past, doesn't mean we won't lose it all back in the future. And don't say we didn't warn you.

Your objective is to ground your team in realism without throwing a wet blanket over the promising potential for future success. I know. Why not just ask you to walk on water? Somebody get on the phone, called Jack Welch (GE) and tell him to get over to your offices right away.

Though the task may seem difficult, and beyond the scope

of your management experience, it's really well within your grasp. The results you hope to achieve are rooted more in attitude than years of experience. Look at all of the experience California Public Employees' Retirement System managers had when they invested $500 million in Enron. After so many years of success, who would dare question their decision to venture into the Texas badlands?

The balance you seek between realism and false invincibility lies in the firm adaptation of three operational principals: exhaustive research, egoless self-evaluation, and moderation of profit expectations. Let's look at all three.

Exhaustive Research

The most productive attitude your team can have in exploring new business opportunities is to assume a posture of ignorance. Throw out all of the assumptions and dig into the available facts. As it turns out, Columbus did not discover America. But preconceived assumptions will surely prevent you from uncovering that fact.

Are computers the wave of the future? Or, is the rudimental act of computing through the Cloud or iPads or Smartphones the actual wave? The experts say we are more calorie-conscious. But Burger King is steadily increasing its sales by offering big, juicy, manly, cheesy, triple deck burgers.

Whether interpolated or presented in plain sight, somewhere in the research lies the truth. Your organization must maintain a commitment to discovering that truth, and avoid bad decisions that will put your company out of business.

Egoless Self-evaluation

"I'm super bad!"

That's part of the lyrics from a popular song by the late, great James Brown.

So it is for many organizations that have experienced consistent success in this turbulent marketplace. The slow creep of confidence has moved team members to the edge of a steep cliff where they stand with perched bodies and extended arms, no doubt in their exalted minds they can fly. Why should tomorrow be any different from yesterday? It's pretty obvious they know their stuff. What idiot is having trouble comprehending the fact they're "super bad"?

"Super bad" teams eventually come to the conclusion they no longer need to follow those drawn-out, mundane practices of due diligence with which mediocre minds have to contend. The smartest guys in the room don't need to waste time reading "scare-tactic" reports submitted to The Securities and Exchange Commission warning that Bernie Madoff is running a ponzi scheme. The man is the former chairman of the NASDAQ stock market. He knows how to make money. He's "super bad" too.

At the point you began to see something magical about your team, that is, you feel you have developed some innate, mystical-like abilities to exploit markets and pick winning outcomes, that's the moment you know you're in trouble. Don't go down that road. Pull back on the reigns. Force your ego back into the cave where it belongs.

Evaluate the capabilities of your team with brutal honesty. Are you really that smart? Can you morph into superior industry experts that quickly? There's a significant learning curve as-sociated with each new market. Sure, you're going to discover opportunities. But it doesn't mean you can march right in and take over. As long as you remind yourself and your team that you're marching onto the field as competitors rather than sure winners, you'll resist the temptation to skip the steps, ultimately resorting to mystical-like decisions. Don't allow your team members to become "super bad."

Moderation of Profit Expectations

In the old days, working as an advertising/marketing consultant for Spec's Liquor Stores in Houston, I learned a great deal from the wise, entrepreneurial-minded owner. He once told me, *"If it looks too good to be true, it probably is."*

What he was saying was the decision to answer the call of greed, pursue fast money and gamble on disproportionately large profits is a formula for disaster. If the market looks too good to be true, it probably is.

Beverage distributors mark up bottled water about 3,000% to grocery stores. Apple has a 50% markup on each iPad. Movie theaters charge an average 1,300% markup on popcorn. But Kroger makes an average 1.5% markup overall on all groceries sold. How do you determine what your profit expectations should be?

The simplest method would be to take the industry's average markup and then add or subtract points based on your strategic advantage or disadvantage in the marketplace. If you enter the US flag market with a monopoly on the colors red, white and blue, your markup is probably going to be more than your competitors. On the other hand, if you enter the soda market against Coke and Pepsi offering only one flavor, I would say forget about the markup. Try to locate the homeless soup line in your neighborhood.

Pursuit of a "reasonable" profit will help to keep you out of trouble. Eventually, when you're up to your eyeballs in cash and can afford to be more aggressive with prevailing risk factors, you might want to roll the dice on an extraordinary opportunity. Until then, remember what old man Spec Jackson of Spec's Liquor Stores, the largest liquor chain in Texas, told me. If it looks too good to be true, it probably is.

Before going inside, there is one final item you need to address. That is the extent to which you're willing to relinquish your better judgment to the process about to take place.

To give an honest answer to this question, we need to define what both entities really mean. Better judgment refers to one's perceived capacity to distinguish the merits of competing options or courses of action.

"The sun is out. But my better judgment tells me it rains a lot this time of year. So despite the apparent evidence of a clear day, I'm going to take an umbrella."

Conversely, the process you are about to pursue, the Anthead Universal Method of Elimination (AUME), doesn't care about your better judgment. What it cares about is an impartial evaluation of the research data. There's a very good chance AUME is going to tell you to do something that feels counterintuitive to your better judgment.

In the late sixties, soldiers returning from Viet Nam brought back many stories of how trusting their gut (better judgment) during combat missions had saved their lives. Even in our modern-day society, law enforcement officials estimate that, without hard evidence, as much as 40% of their decision-making is based on gut feelings.

In his book, *Intuition: Its Powers and Perils,* psychology Professor Davis Myers says, *"Our gut intuitions are terrific at some things, such as instantly reading emotions in others' faces, but not so good at others, such as guessing about the stock market, assessing risks and predicting football outcomes. A hunch might be the result of overconfidence in our own abilities or knowledge, or a faulty or reconstructed memory"*.

The Anthead Universal Method of Elimination, however, is based on the Wisdom of the Mound. But as we established earlier, the "wisdom" itself can be corrupted by unclean data, missing components or a lack of representation by certain universes. Was Osama bin Laden hiding in a cave or not? And where did the data come from that said he was?

What it really comes down to is your belief that the old system of management is dead and the Anthead System is the one you've chosen to take its place. In Las Vegas they say, "All bets in." It means there's no room to straddle the fence. Either you're in or out. This is what you need to decide before you go into the meeting.

At noon the conference room is buzzing with excitement. Team members have brought their own laptops, tablets, iPhones and old fashion legal pads, chunked with notes. A lively discussion is already taking place over the volatility of hybrid vehicles. You almost need a gavel to get everyone's attention.

You say: Looks like we're in for a wild ride today. I wouldn't have it any other way. Before we get into the heart of our discussion, I need to ask if anything has changed or been discovered over the last twenty-four hours that would alter the current listing on the board?

Larvae Daily says: Yes. I had recommended In-Home Senior Care as a possible business to look at; and I still think it has a lot of potential. But I happened to be talking to my sister last night and she's going for an interview with Amedisys Home Health. They already have a large footprint all over the state. But they're hiring and expanding, trying to get ready for a new national in-home healthcare competitor that's coming into Texas next year. So I think we should just take that one down.

You say: Anyone disagree?

Drone Howard says: Actually, I heard a similar rumor. A friend of mine in real estate told me some big healthcare conglomerate was buying up property in Houston, Austin and San Antonio, planning to enter the Texas market next year. Could be the same company.

You say: Okay, let's take it down. Good save, Ms Daily. But I'm going to put my new recommendation in your spot. After finishing up the initial research, I believed the manufacture and distribution of custom toilets deserves a look. The industry is exploding and no one dominates the market so far. We might have a shot.

You erase in-home healthcare and replace it with toilet distribution. Now comes the hard part. It's time to introduce AUME to the rest of the team.

The Anthead Universal Method of Elimination

The Anthead Universal Method of Elimination (AUME) is the official decision-making matrix for the Anthead System. Similar to other business matrixes, AUME attempts to sort through existing options to determine which will offer the most desirable outcome. In the process, the most undesirable options are eliminated. I say "most" because, in many cases, some undesirable options end up sticking around as a backup plan just in case new information or influential variables such as titanium dioxide dust prevent the primary option from being executed.

Let's say you're lost in the forest with family and friends. From a high ridge you can see three trails that lead into town. Trail one leads through a dense thicket teeming with poisonous snakes, spiders, wolves and black bear. Trail two is over a raging river fill with crocodiles. The crossing is a rotten rope bridge that's swaying, precariously, in the wind. Trail three stretches over a steep mountain range requiring some intense climbing and physical toughness, which means your mother-in-law who has arthritis and swollen joints will have to be left behind.

Now you're thinking, *Why did I waste your time talking about trails one and two? Trail three is the best choice on so many different levels.*

In reality (and with regained composure), using the AUME matrix, options three would be the first to go away. The weighted value placed on saving everyone's life would far exceed the convenience of leaving your dear mother-in-law behind. Weighted values, overriding priorities and acknowledged imperfect outcomes are what AUME is all about.

Let's say you own a couple of mobile fast food Tex-Mex trucks. You ride around to different office buildings, car lots and construction sites selling taco, fajitas, tortillas, and other stir-fried peppered delights. While gassing up one of your trucks, a man approaches you and asks that you begin coming around to his construction sites during the lunch hour to service his workers. As it turns out, the man is the owner of a large construction company with multiple developments in progress. By the end of the year, his locations are generating 50% of your business.

One day he pulls you off to the side and asks if you would

give his son a job for the summer. He feels the high school senior is spoiled and lazy. The dad wants him to experience the real world outside the confines of his father's protective umbrella. "I want you to let him sweat over those hot stoves in your trucks and ride around with no air-conditioning. I don't want him to think that life is going to be easy just because I'm his father."

You agree to hire him at minimum wage, which is no strain to you since your once fledgling business has started to grow. The boy is only going to be there three months during the summer and then return to school to finish his senior year. It's the least you can do for a customer who has helped to increase your business by 50%.

As it turns out, the boy is the lazy, rebellious, late for work, snippy with customers, continually complaining to other employees about working conditions, and totally disinterested in learning the basic essentials necessary to do the job.

Here's the clincher. Without asking permission and having only a beginner's license in his wallet, he rams one of your trucks into a parked Lincoln Navigator at one of the car lots you service. The dealer is fiery mad, the insurance is going to go up, and for the rest of that day, the business normally generated by that truck is lost. There's no doubt in your mind. The boy has to go.

Or does he?

Under the Anthead System, you put everything into perspective using the AUME decision matrix. You assign a weighted value to all variables and allow the numeric totals to select the most plausible outcome.

In a very simplified scenario I might assign a possible maximum weighted score of 100 to all desired outcomes. On a scale of 1 to 100, how important would it be to:

DESIRED OUTCOME	WEIGHT
Prevent future accidents	80
Keep the boy away from customers	50
Keep the boy from influencing other employees	60
Teach the boy a lesson on the consequences of being late and slacking off	35
Avoid jeopardizing 50% of your company's business as a result of alienating the boy's father	99

Even though you're outraged at the boy's conduct and would like to fire him on the spot, the AUME decision matrix has identified the outcome most important to you ... **protecting the 50% increase in your business.** Now you must look at the options that have the greatest possibility of leading to that outcome.

OPTIONS FOR DESIRED OUTCOME	WEIGHT
Take away the boy's responsibilities and leave him in the back of the truck.	70
Tell the father the boy is a hopeless case and pray he understands your frustration.	35
Reason with the boy to change his ways.	50
Keep everything the same except for truck keys and try to ride out the summer.	95

The assignment of weights is based on the Wisdom of the Mound. You've had a chance to observe the father up close and personal. Some of his employees have informed you he has a fiery temper and is sometimes illogical in his thought process. They've also heard through the grapevine the boy had gone to several high-priced counselors without rendering any change in his attitude. Thus, through your informal research, you've concluded that talking to the father is too risky (a 65% chance he will seek retribution). And talking to the boy is a waste of time. What would you say with such profound meaning that the counselors haven't already said?

If Larvae Daily were involved in the decision-making, she would place a much higher value on the boy's future; a lot less on profitability. To have the boy come back ten years later and say, "You know what? The care, concern and tough love you showed for me when I rode on your Tex-Mex trucks was the turning point in my life. I just graduated from medical school and wanted to come back to say thank you."

The consistently high value she places on human capital is an invaluable balancing mechanism in your organization. That's why it's so critical to have all universes represented in the decision-making process. There will be potential outcomes for which you won't bother to look and skewed weighted values that reflect only your narrow profit agenda if you don't involve other team members in the process.

In this simple scenario, look how easy it was to eliminate all options that didn't lead directly to your profit objective. This is exactly how, Chick-Fil-A, FedEx, Ben & Jerry's and Google would beat you in the marketplace. Based on their mission statements and core values, they would've felt compelled to develop an extraordinary, painstaking rehabilitation program for the young man including Teen Boot Camp, Scared-Straight prison visits, Christian retreats, overseas family exchanges, peer-group mentoring from college student, and so on. Then you would've read in the newspaper the father's construction company had invested $50 million in FedEx's Tex-Mex trucks with a bold plan to take the concept nationwide. You would've been left with the perplexing question, "Why do these kinds of competitors always come out on top?"

This is the essence of synthetical thinking, except with a more complex twist. Everything matters. But when deployed through the use of the AUME decision matrix, some things matter more than others. AUME expects you to tell it what matters most through the use of weighted numerical values. Then it will tell you which options are best.

AUME is different from most decision matrixes in that it drills all the way down to the execution level to examine the potential for each team member's existing capabilities to morph into a meaningful contributive mode. If you're going to operate a nuclear plant, AUME wants to know which one of your team members is going in to check the deadly breeder reactors and control rods; and which member will write the complex reports to send to the government.

In the Anthead System, the key to successful morphing lies in the organization's ability to accurately evaluate its team. What are each team member's current competencies, that is, experience, training, attitude, preferences, aptitude or business Intelligence Quotient and trustworthiness? And what will it take in terms of time and money to get the team where it needs to be?

In a normal ant mound, the larger ants morph from worker to scouts to soldier/protectors. Their larger bodies allowed them to withstand unexpected attacks while searching for food outside the mound. But if the mount is under attack, those same large bodies are used to plug holes in the mound so advancing armies cannot get inside. The Queen knows they're morphing capabilities. She does not ask them to become a larvae sacrifice.

If AUME determines you have no big-bodied soldiers and

no one capable of morphing to that position, then it re-focuses on the question of how much in terms of time and money is it going to take to get the team where it needs to be. Too much time and/or too much money points to a hole too big to plug ... alone, that is. You could decide to explore a new set of options which facilitate joint ventures, mergers, strategic partnerships and associations, or some innovative approach to creative financing. That's what the big oil companies do when they form billion dollar partnerships to drill high-risk wells. In the end, however, the decision may come down to a sobering admission of facts: You are in no shape to exploit the market and have to move on.

The best way to understand the power of AUME is to jump right in and apply it. You have eleven potential markets on the board ready to be chosen or eliminated or relegated to the bench until one of the starters gets knocked out.

Start with your parking lot objective of grounding the team in realism.

You say: I don't expect you to grasp this concept the first time around. But as we repeat the process, I promise you'll get the hang of it and wonder how we ever got along without it. Now let's plug the information in for option #1.

Here's the diagram:

Figure 1: AUME Decision Matrix

The Anthead Universal Method of Elimination©

Small Business Decision Matrix under Anthead System

(AUME) Decision Matrix

	Possible Score	Final Score
Name: **New Market Entry - 2012** — Final Option **#11**	**6391**	**6214**

Description: Decision matrix to identify plausibility of entering new markets.

Team	Owner	Howard	Maria	Wayne	Mike	Bradford	Daily	Sally	Ortega	Tech1	Tech2	Riley	New Hire
Ant Contribution	Management/ High level sales	Management/ Day-to-day oper.	Administrative/ Order taking and custom fragrances	Sales/ Government and health related bells & whistles	Sales Mgmt/ Coord. major presentation, locate distr., old order	Systems architecture/ new tools software, sales and support	Finding health and elderly facilities/ Giveaway press cam.	Sales/ Corporate and real estate plus bells & whistles	Deliveries/ Other as needed	Production/ Innovation	Production/ Innovation	Production/ Innovation	Accounting/ Creative Financing and acquisitions
Competency Rating	90	95	75	80	80	85	90	85	95	75	75	75	90
Make-Ready Time / Cost	180 days / $4000	90 days / $500	240 days / $5000	90 days / $1000	90 days / $8000	240 days / $16000	90 days / $3000	60 days / $500	30 days / $800	90 days / $1000	90 days / $1000	90 days / $1000	30 days / $15000

Key Performance Variables	Weight	Option#1	Option#2	Option#3	Option#4	Option#5	Option#6	Option#7	Option#8	Option#9	Option#10	Option#11
		Raw / Wgtd	Raw / Wgtd	Raw / Wgtd	Raw / Wgtd	Raw / Wgtd	Raw / Wgtd	Raw / Wgtd	Raw / Wgtd	Raw / Wgtd	Raw / Wgtd	Raw / Wgtd
Strategic Performance Variables	1-10											
Matches existing organizational core values	10	85/850	90/900	92/920	80/800	90/900	90/900	70/700	88/880	95/950	95/950	88/800
Manageable initial cost to enter market	8	40/320	75/600	99/792	99/792	80/640	70/560	80/640	60/480	99/792	95/760	95/760
Attractive return on investment/Profit margins	7	70/490	90/630	80/560	40/280	70/490	65/455	80/560	70/490	60/420	85/595	90/630
High level of team interest/buy-in	7	45/315	50/350	60/420	25/175	80/560	25/175	15/105	90/630	90/630	92/644	70/490
Ease of exit when market plays out	5	30/150	85/425	90/450	95/475	75/375	35/175	45/225	40/200	90/450	85/425	93/465
Tactical Performance Variables	-	-	-	-	-	-	-	-	-	-	-	-
Able to compete and protect/Barriers	9	1/9	70/630	65/585	10/90	50/450	50/450	65/585	10/90	50/450	65/585	70/630
Opportunity to differentiate/Add Bells & Whistles	7	99/693	99/693	80/560	60/420	25/175	65/455	55/385	40/280	60/420	35/245	99/693
Government intervention in our favor	6	50/300	50/300	35/210	40/240	90/540	1/6	85/510	99/594	99/594	99/594	90/540
Operational Performance Variables	-	-	-	-	-	-	-	-	-	-	-	-
Reasonable learning curve for existing personnel	5	1/5	10/50	80/400	97/485	90/450	85/425	90/450	70/350	90/450	90/450	90/450
Ample outside resources and vendors	4	99/396	99/396	90/360	85/340	90/360	85/340	90/360	50/200	90/360	80/320	90/360
Current operation adds to competitive advantage	4	1/4	1/4	1/4	40/160	80/320	70/140	45/180	70/280	10/40	99/396	99/396
Total Weighted Score		**3532**	**4978**	**5261**	**4257**	**5260**	**4081**	**4700**	**4474**	**5556**	**5964**	**6214**

Note: You may view this in color at: http://antheadsystem.com/AUME.html. If asked, the password is AUME.

Let's make the diagram larger ... just in case there are any ole timers out there with thick specs like mine.

The Anthead Universal Method of Elimination©

Small Business Decision Matrix under Anthead System

(AUME) Decision Matrix

Possible Score	Final Score
6391	6214

Name: New Market Entry - 2012

Final Option #11

Description: Decision matrix to identify plausibility of entering new markets.

Team	Owner	Howard	Maria	Wayne	Mike	Bradford	Daily	Sally	Ortega	Tech1	Tech2	Riley	New Hire
Ant Contribution	Management/ High-level sales	Management/ Day-to-day oper.	Administrative/ Order-taking and custom fragrances	Sales/Government bells & wheels	Sales/Government and health-related bells & wheels	Systems architecture, and health-related major presentation, sales and support	Finding health and elderly facilities/ Giveaway press cam	Sales/Corporate and real estate plus bells & wheels	Deliveries/Other as needed	Production/ Innovation	Production/ Innovation	Production/ Innovation	Accounting/ Creative Financing and acquisitions
Competency Rating	90	95	75	80	80	85	90	85	95	75	75	75	90
Make-Ready Time / Cost	180 days / $4000	90 days / $4000	240 days / $5000	90 days / $1000	90 days / $8000	240 days / $10,000	90 days / $3000	60 days / $560	90 days / $8800	90 days / $1000	90 days / $1000	90 days / $1000	90 days / $15,000 (Add to mentoring reserve)

Key Performance Variables	Weight	Option#1 Cloud Comp	Option#2 Home Svc Apps	Option#3 Patent Darbie	Option#4 Aging Products	Option#5 Diamond Tools	Option#6 Green Haul	Option#7 Precision Tools	Option#8 Elec Battery Hub	Option#9 Energy Center	Option#10 LT Plastic Parts	Option#11 Custom Trailers
	1-10	Raw / Wgtd	Raw / Wgtd	Raw / Wgtd	Raw / Wgtd	Raw / Wgtd	Raw / Wgtd	Raw / Wgtd	Raw / Wgtd	Raw / Wgtd	Raw / Wgtd	Raw / Wgtd
Strategic Performance Variables												
Matches existing organizational core values	10	85/850	90/900	92/920	80/800	90/900	90/900	70/700	88/880	95/950	95/950	88/800
Manageable initial cost to enter market	8	40/320	75/600	99/792	99/792	80/640	70/560	80/640	60/480	99/792	95/760	95/760
Attractive return on investment/Profit margins	7	70/490	90/630	80/560	40/280	70/490	65/455	80/560	70/490	60/420	85/595	90/630
High level of team interest/buy-in	7	45/315	50/350	60/420	25/175	80/560	25/175	15/105	90/630	90/630	92/644	70/490
Ease of exit when market plays out	5	30/150	85/425	90/450	95/475	75/375	35/175	45/225	40/200	90/450	85/425	93/465
Tactical Performance Variables												
Able to compete and protect/Barriers	9	1/9	70/630	65/585	10/90	50/450	50/450	65/585	10/90	50/450	65/585	70/630
Opportunity to differentiate/Add Bells & Whistles	7	99/693	99/693	80/560	60/420	25/175	65/455	55/385	40/280	60/420	35/245	99/693
Government intervention in our favor	6	50/300	50/300	35/210	40/240	90/540	1/6	85/510	99/594	99/594	99/594	90/540
Operational Performance Variables												
Reasonable learning curve for existing personnel	5	1/5	10/50	80/400	97/485	90/450	85/425	90/450	70/350	90/450	90/450	90/450
Ample outside resources and vendors	4	99/396	99/396	90/360	85/340	90/360	85/340	90/360	50/200	90/360	80/320	90/360
Current operation adds to competitive advantage	4	1/4	1/4	1/4	40/160	80/320	70/140	45/180	70/280	10/40	99/396	99/396
Total Weighted Score		3532	4978	5261	4257	5260	4081	4700	4474	5556	5964	6214

To become familiar with AUME's decision-making process, we should first look at the fundamental structure of the matrix and then the content within. And yes, these next seven pages are the most challenging in the entire book ... like reading how to ride a bike. But don't quit. You'll get it!

The AUME Decision Matrix is comprised of two sections. Section One or the top section is essentially the summary section offering the results of your team's painstaking research and decision-making, which has already transpired in Section Two. Section One is similar to a company's profit and loss statement highlighting the bare bone values that represent the organization's cumulative effort behind the scenes. Section One offers a comprehensive snapshot of the end game, but could not exist without the numerical heavy lifting accomplished in Section Two.

Let's look at the components of Section One:

- **Name** ... the name identifying this particular decision matrix. Under the Anthead System, you'll be using multiple matrixes supporting multiple decisions and need to be able to quickly distinguish one from the other.

- **Description** ... elaborates, to a greater extent, on the reason the matrix is being used.

- **Final Option Arrow** ... identifies the final option selected by the matrix and points to the resulting scores.

- **Possible Score** ... represents the highest possible numeric value a particular option could have achieved. You could think of this as a "perfect world" score.

- **Final Score** ... represents the actual score earned by the option that AUME has recommended. This score is important in that it not only shows how close the selection came to an Appreciative Inquiry "dream state" of ideal circumstances, but also reflects an apple-to-apple numerical comparison to competing options that lost out in the process.

- **Team** ... the team row identifies all team members associated with the plan or decision. There may be other team members in the organization which have nothing to do with this particular decision. Those members are excluded from this matrix.

- **Ant (anticipated) Contribution** ... this row offers a top level summary of the anticipated contribution for which each team member will be held accountable. This is particularly helpful in identifying the morphing range of each participant. The summary is derived from a Team Member Contribution Worksheet which presents the morphing aspect in more detail.

- **Competency Rating** ... this is the numeric value that represents each team member's current ability to function effectively within the chosen option. In many ways, it's a snapshot of a team member's functionality with an action plan for improvement. So if team member A is a doctor and the chosen option requires medics in Iraq, his competency rating might be a 90. But if team member B is a doctor and has experience in combat from the Gulf War, her rating might be a 99. This information also flows out of the Team Member Contribution Worksheet

- **Make-ready** ... represents the strategic steps anticipated to move each team member to the desired level of competence or functionality. This information flows out of a Make-Ready Intervention Worksheet that identifies team members requiring intervention and associated costs. (See page 224)

As mentioned earlier, Section Two or the bottom section focuses on the meticulous process of evaluating the merits of each option. Like most decision matrixes, the key performance variables are assigned a numerical weight based on their importance to a given outcome. Then these variables are plugged into each option to see which combination generates the highest score. Stick with me. This is going to be a piece of cake.

Here are the components for Section Two:

- **Key Performance Variables** ... represent the priorities that need to be satisfied in order to produce a desired outcome. If you wanted to go swimming but didn't have any transportation, a key performance variable might be the availability of a large body of water within walking distance. Key performance variables are conditions that point to an end game or desired outcome that you would like to see occur.

Using this particular AUME decision matrix, key performance variables are divided into three categories: **strategic, tactical and operational.**

- **Strategic Key Performance Variables** ... represent the long-term, high-level umbrella requirements that need to be met in order for the outcome to take place. Maybe a church has some money and wants to invest in a business. A strategic requirement might be no liquor, gambling or illegal activity. So much for that double-your-money business deal in Las Vegas. Or, the variable needing to be met might be as simple as a guaranteed return of 5% on investment. This is a high-level parameter that dictates which actions can be taken at a lower level to achieve the desired outcome.

- **Tactical Key Performance Variables** ... represent the mid-range choices associated with deployment options such as whether to travel by ship or plane or whether to sell books in paperback or ebook formats. A woman might decide to wear a certain dress to the office because of a formal meeting. That decision represents a chosen tactic to accomplish a higher goal of being noticed or getting promoted. The operational phase comes into play when she puts the exact dress on.

- **Operational Key Performance Variables** ... represent the lowest level, day-to-day options that carry out upper-level decisions. As mentioned earlier, the act of putting on the exact dress and finding accessories to go with it would be operational. Asking a specific employee to work overtime or shooting the enemy in war would also be of an operational nature.

- **Weight** ... represents the numerical value given to a key performance variable based on its perceived importance to the overall outcome. I might determine that gasoline is a key performance variable in getting my car to the store (desired outcome) and might assign it a weight of 9 out of a possible range of 1-10. I might also assign a weight of 1 to clean tires and 2 to the radio working properly. But if my teenage daughter is riding with me and has input in the value assignments, she might raise the radio value to 7.

Assigning weight to key performance variables is neither arbitrary nor precise. Under the Anthead System, assigned weights flow out of a consensus among team members in an open forum.

The more you're able to get team members to agree on the accuracy and objectivity of assigned weights and numerical values, the more obligated they become to buy into the outcome. Several years ago, I was part of a team meeting where a lady was all for the process. Then, at the end, when she realized her option had lost out, she began a tirade against the validity of the process. It's important at every step to eliminate or the least minimize any wiggle room that would allow a team member to back out.

- **Options** ... list all options under consideration by the team. This is not to say a new option could not be formulated from a combination of existing choices.

Let's say you're trying to get to Canada on a limited budget. The initial options from which you have to choose include driving, flying, railway, and the bus. After exploring all of the existing options, however, you might create a final option which involves flying into Minnesota using a special discount pass, then catching the bus from there to Canada. This final option would be considered the "best of the best". It completely satisfies your stated objective, and yet, it was not originally among the selections.

This is the beauty of the AUME Decision Matrix. It offers both structure and flexibility on the fly, without contaminating the process.

- **Raw/Weighted Values** ... represent raw, baseline numerical values assigned to a key variable under that particular option, as well as the final value after the weighted importance of that variable has been applied. I know. This concept is more easily shown than described. Just know that Lady Gaga might receive a maximum value of 10 lying around the pool in a bikini. But if you're holding on to a rope on the side of a mountain and need a strong, burly weightlifter to pull you up, her raw value of 10, weighted by the circumstances, is going to go way down.

- **Total Weighted Score** ... represents the cumulative weighted score for that particular option. In other words, all of the variables have spoken and this is what the option is worth.

221

Notice the cumulative "raw score" is not listed. That's because in the end, the weight's influence on the raw score is what counts. Lady Gaga's raw score means nothing to you if you're preoccupied with a free-fall down the mountainside. At that point, you're only interested in the bottom line.

Now that you've been introduced to the components that drive the AUME Matrix, let's talk a bit more about procedure. It's really not that complicated. You pull your team together, enter an Appreciative Inquiry (AI) dream state that reflects the ideal outcome you want to achieve, identify the key performance variables that will lead to that outcome, and give each variable a weighted numerical value based on the priorities tied to the outcome. The final step is to plug in the options to see which one scores the highest.

In this case, the AI dream state points to a new market opportunity that satisfies all of the key performance variables. We'll look at a number of options to determine why they were selected or discarded by your team. But first, let's take a few minutes to discuss some best practices associated with the process.

Take a look at the column in Section Two labeled "*Weight*". You'll notice the numbers range from 1-10, meaning the most important variables receive a maximum score of 10, while the least important receive a 1. This numerical range is pretty straightforward and coincides with the average non-technical, non-business perception of value. Quite often we hear men say, "She's a ten," or women say, "That movie was a ten." The whole point of selecting this numerical range is to keep things simple for all team members, as well as present an easy-to-discern, visual separation between the numerical range use to express *weights*, and the numerical range used to express the "*raw value*" of a particular option.

As you can see, the numerical range assigned to *options*

is from 1-100, which is the same familiar range teachers use in school. This range offers a subconscious baseline perception that synchronizes all numbers in a historical or traditional kind of hierarchy. All of our teachers taught us that 90-100 was a good thing. So when we look at the matrix and see an assigned value of 93, no further explanation is required.

Beyond that, I immediately realize that 93 is a *"raw value"* and not a *"weight"* value. Some matrixes use 1-10 as a weight range and 1-10 as a raw value range for options as well. Though the calculations may produce the same accuracy, I strongly disagree in choosing a duplicate range that could foster unnecessary confusion. Remember, under the Anthead Systems all relevant members of the team (salespersons, secretaries, truck drivers, etc.) are viewing the matrix. The last thing you want to do is confuse or discourage members from participating.

Think about it this way. That long number is your credit card number. But the expiration date is not going to be more than a two-digit month and four-digit year. You know it right away.

Finally, and most impressive is the way the weighted scores stands out from the rest of the crowd. Without having a finance degree from Harvard, I realize the *"big numbers"* like 900 and 792, the ones that have been baptized by weight, are the ones that really matter. Still, I can check the raw scores (which are color-coded in real life and online) to see if a particular option has, in my opinion, been short-changed.

One last best practice and then we'll move on.

A great deal of the information provided in Section One flows out of supplementary worksheets that you and the drone/enforcer develop. Once the final option has been chosen by the team, it's a good idea to have these worksheets on hand and available to each member of the team during follow-up sessions.

These worksheets don't have to be elaborate. In fact, the simpler the better. The whole idea is to capture a more comprehensive understanding of each person's role, level of empowerment, and anticipated responsibilities. The more team members know about their impact within a chosen option, the more effective they're going to be in reaching their desired goals.

MAKE-READY INTERVENTION WORKSHEET

Name	Task	Intervention	Cost
Jones, Riley	Oven Supervision	Advance training	$1000
McCall, Sally	Sales to Hm Developers	Dues to join real estate assoc.	$500
Sanchez, Maria	Old plastic plus manage toilet accessories	Fragrance sales training	$5000
Howard, Jake	Master industry trends	Dues to join Am. Restroom Assoc	$500

TEAM MEMBER CONTRIBUTION WORKSHEET

Anticipated Performance Range

OPTION **11**	Manufacture and Distribution of Custom Toilets

Readiness Appraisal

Overall Score: 90 /100

Employee No. - J3292

Name:	Hines, Bradford	Job Title:	IT Manager
Department:	IT Department	Supervisor	HOWARD

Evaluation Date: 03-22-2012

ı Summary of Responsibilities

Bradford's anticipated contribution to the new market entry will consist of realigning existing systems architecture to support all activities associated with the manufacture and distribution of Averest custom toilets which will include but not be limited to admin, sales, financial, warehouse production activities, procurement tracking, shipping and customer service activities.

Assessment of Readiness

Performance Assessment:
EE - Exceeds Expectations
ME - Meets Expectations
NI - Needs Improvement to Meet Expectations

Performance Measures

Score: 90 /100

Competency	Performance Assessment EE	ME	NI	Comments:	Score/3.0
Application Development/Support Proficiency in realigning systems to support new activities and provide additional functionality for all departments transitioning to new market pursuit.	●	○	○	Exceptional performance in previous years	95
Business Analysis Proficiency in anticipating market innovation that would reduce costs and extend the value of hardware and software acquisitions needed to support the expansion of the company's overall operation.	○	●	○	Should do fine but may require some additional technical training in warehouse hookup.	85

225

A case in point would be the row under the Make-Ready Intervention Worksheet (page 196) that shows Maria's anticipated contribution. Under chosen Option #11, she'll be expected to morph from her current administrative/receptionist duties to a primary sales order-taker for existing customers still needing to be serviced, as well as manage the distribution of toilet accessories such as soaps, sprays and scented paper packaged with the units. Although you don't plan to continue selling plastic utility toolboxes and CD/DVD covers, the process of phasing out existing product lines will be gradual, which means someone will have to service old customers until they find new suppliers. What an excellent training ground for your future CEO.

Another smart business move might be to meet with a respectable, trustworthy competitor to hand over your customer lists and receive a flat fee or percentage of profits for a designated period of time. Meanwhile, using the Intervention worksheet, Maria's participation and additional responsibilities (and earnings) during the transition must be made crystal clear.

The worksheets should provide all of this information, that is, to the extent that it doesn't create resentment or push team members into a defensive mode. A precautionary measure would be to meet with each team member privately to alert them of your realignment plans. That way, you are able to minimize the chances for any unwanted surprises during follow-up sessions and offer each member of the team a preliminary vote of confidence in their ability to make a meaningful contribution.

Now, the fun part begins. In the final chapter, we'll get a chance to see the power of AUME in action. With a general idea of the procedure and how each component works, let's plug in a few selected options and bring the whole process to life. Tighten your seat belts for a downhill thriller. It's going to be a fantastic ride.

CHAPTER

9

Case Study - The Conclusion

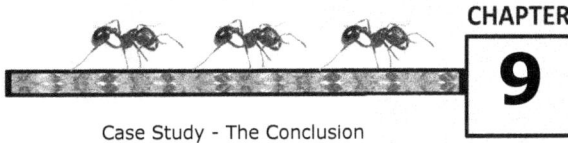

*F*or the purpose of this writing, we're going to look at the action after the fact, with the expert infallibility of a Monday morning quarterback. In doing so, we are able to expedite our evaluation process and avoid the mundane blow-by-blow recordings of who said what. Close our eyes and count to three. And when you open them again, imagine the selection process is complete. Now you and I can spend our time looking at what team members did, why they did it and how it will impact our desired outcomes. The heavy lifting is over. Our job will be to simply evaluate the results.

We start with Cloud Computing.

OPTION #1

Cloud Computing

Cloud computing is any sold-on-demand subscription-based or

pay-per-use internet service that increases storage capacity and/or access to software applications without investing in new infrastructure, training or software licensing. Growing an average of 32% annually, these services fall into three categories: Infrastructure-Services, Platform-Services and Software-Services. Users need nothing more than a personal computer and internet access to take advance of these services.

Businesses worldwide are stampeding to the cloud; over 60% of all global companies indicate a readiness to embrace cloud computing over the next five years. Since 2008, cloud computing trademark filings have increased by 483%. Seven of ten CIOs in the US, UK, Japan and South Korea named cloud implementation as a top priority. Heavy-hitters such as Amazon, Dell, HP, Google, Rackspace, IBM, Microsoft and Oracle have jumped into the market with both feet, spending billions on technological research and development and aggressive promotions to position themselves as market leaders. The market is red hot and looks to stay that way for the next five to seven years.

So why did the Averest team turn it down?

A closer look at the AUME matrix shows the strengths and weaknesses of the option, variable by variable. Let go right down the line.

Key Performance Variable

Matches existing organizational core values

This is huge, a high level requirement with a weight of 10. It reflects the organization's core beliefs and reason for existing.

Perhaps, at this point, it would be good to take a step back and look at your organization's mission statement. That's where your reason for existing should be found.

Averest Plastic Enterprises Mission Statement

Produce and distribute products and services that wow our customers and give our team members a strong sense of accomplishment, reinforcing their belief that what they do really matters.

High-tech worker Bradford's cloud option didn't do badly in this category. In fact an 85 from my old college history professor would've been good reason to go out and paint the town with a couple of ice cold kegs. The only option that didn't score well in this category was Option #7: Prisoner Transport. The need was there and the market was growing. However, the team felt nothing in the prisoner process pointed back to a strong sense of accomplishment that reinforced the group's belief that what they would be doing really mattered. Cloud computing offered a much greater appeal.

Key Performance Variable

Manageable initial cost to enter the market

In this category, also important with a weight of 8, Option #1 failed miserably. Most entrepreneurs go into business with the understanding that it takes money to make money. Some type of investment is inevitable. But each organization has its limits, which means without the necessary funding to enter a market, as promising as it may seem, that market is off limits to that particular organization.

With this option, the funding barrier reared its ugly head in the form of massive infrastructure of storage servers, proprietary software, licensing agreements and technical expertise. In a hot market the cost of hiring technical experts grows exponentially, as in the case of web developers and programmers during the early

90's. In this case, technicians with cloud computing experience were found to be in short supply, and by Bradford's own admission, prong to go with larger companies that paid top dollar and offered a chance for advancement. Beyond that, internet data centers and hosting companies appeared to be the fastest growing segment in the industry even before the rush to the cloud materialized. Mobile services were already driving the growth. According to Intel's calculations, an extra server was needed for every 600 Smartphones and 122 tablet computers sold. Additionally, the research showed Google operated over a million servers, Facebook 30,000, with the need to acquire more each month. That translated into an accelerating cost of buying servers for years to come. With $600,000 in the bank and a $250,000 line of credit, there was no way Averest Plastic Enterprises could handle that kind of extraordinary cover charge to get inside the Cloud.

Key Performance Variable

Attractive return on investment/Profit margins

In this category, Option #1 was passing, but barely. One of the team members pulled up an article quoting Microsoft chief software architect Ray Ozzie telling stakeholders to expect much lower margins on cloud computing services; nothing close to the 79% profit margins traditional software products such as Windows and Office brought in. Amazon also reported slimming operating margins in the cloud, although they didn't reveal the exact markup on sales revenue. But offering the Amazon EC2 Micro Instance service free for a year certainly didn't help.

Team members felt the classic "over-supplied" market scenario was unfolding among providers. Inevitably, as more players enter a market, prices go down, taking margins with them, until a shakeout leaves only a few deep-pocket competitors still standing. In the expanding world of cloud computing, revenue was climbing, but actual profit margins were going down. This wasn't a place that Averest needed to be.

High level of team interest/buy-in

Tell the kids you're taking them to Disney World and watch them roll all over the floor. Tell the kids you're taking them to see the Oklahoma City Philharmonic Orchestra and watch them ... roll all over the floor. It's a different roll, however, with kicking, whining and kid-swearing. The general feeling is "you can make us go. But we don't have to like it".

Each team has a collective conscience with unifying beliefs that influence its openness to recommendations and strategic courses of action. The primary reason Option #1 received a failing grade of 45 was the team's perception that Option #1 was tech-heavy and more suited for a young Bill Gates and company.

When you look at current team competencies with an eye on rating team members based on their technological expertise, you quickly discover that Bradford is the only member remotely qualified to pursue an organizational realignment with emphasis on the Cloud. In other words, technology is not your company's strong suit.

There's really nothing wrong with this, as low tech companies such as Handi Quilter in Utah, manufacturer of quilting machines, and Oak Tree Dairy in Long Island, vertically integrated producer and distributor of over three hundred dairy products, have both demonstrated. There's an unlimited potential for low-tech businesses to be very successful. It's simply a matter of choosing to pursue markets that match existing competencies, or replacing key team members in order to pursue a high tech market. Since you're happy with your current team and the synergy that already exists, observing the lack of buying-in among current team members is just another reason to eliminate Option #1.

Ease of exit when market plays out

In this category, Option #1 also received a failing grade of 30. It's really a no-brainer to envision the continued rapid technological innovation in cloud computing, leaving you holding a warehouse full of antiquated servers that no one wants to buy. It's like trying to resell a jump (flash) drive that holds one gigabyte of storage. They were so cool when they first came out. Now jump drives hold 128 gigs and up.

Exiting the market would be painful, a pain your team is not willing to endure.

Able to compete and protect/Barriers

This category, with a weighted value of 9, is extremely important. And yet, sadly, Option #1 received the lowest possible score: 1. With Amazon, Dell, Google and Microsoft already in the market and firmly committed to staying there, Averest doesn't stand a chance. Having said that, I quickly rush to stick an asterisk at the end of this sentence.

Just because the heavy-hitters are already in the market doesn't mean you can't find a successful niche. Silicon Valley computer manufacturer SeaMicro is successfully competing against heavyweight server makers such as HP, Dell and IBM with the superior technology of a low-powered custom-tailored server that operates more efficiently and cost much less to own. VirnetX, an internet networking and security company, has pursued a successful market strategy of multiple patents and strict litigation, recently obtaining a $200 million settlement against Microsoft for patent infringement.

The problem with Averest is it has nothing to bring to the table in the way of superior technology, innovation or litigation. The barriers are insurmountable for Averest with no entry point in sight.

Key Performance Variable

Opportunity to differentiate/Add Bells & Whistles

Option #1 received a 99 in this category. Cloud computing offers an array of differentiation opportunities that go far beyond the basic setup. Providers are able to offer a full range of hardware, software and security services, including technical support capable of reaching deep into a customer's organization with custom service packages and programs that drag along the masses of late adapters into the cumulus light. There's even a meta-cloud (cloud for the clouds) to seamlessly tie all networks together.

If Averest were somehow able to get into the market, this ability to differentiate would be critical in averting the dreaded strategy of competing based exclusively on price. But with Option #1 fading into oblivion, that awaiting opportunity is really all for naught.

Government intervention in our favor

Option #1 received a neutral score of 50 in this category. Government policy has little influence or negative impact on strategies designed to compete in the cloud.

In discussing government policy and potential intervention into the marketplace, my initial thought was to state the facts and move on. Unfortunately, I found that option to be somewhat contrary to my stated mission for writing the book. **Thus, into more deep waters we plunge.**

Government intervention is a hot potato with strong opinions on both sides of the issue. Some gurus of commerce say government should not interfere with the business process. The markets have a way of taking care of themselves. Still others say government has an obligation to intervene when business policies threaten the system and the economy as a whole.

In evaluating the extremely complex, ever-evolving world of microeconomic, interrelated, interdependent systems that link powerful monopolies, oligopolies and duopolies across the globe; those multinational conglomerates that can transfer trillions of dollars at the speed of light, create wealth, real and illusory, terminate billions of workers, bring down entire governments and pollute the stratosphere so badly that Mother Nature, herself, is on the run, I have come to a crystal clear, indisputable conclusion. Both sides are right.

Having owned a small business for many years, I can remember countless hours of frustration dealing with government forms, red tape and bureaucratic stumbling blocks that pulled me away from my core, profit-making activities. I had the IRS freeze my accounts and never admit any wrong-doing, the state try to collect sales taxes on exempt nontaxable services, and costly mis-information from government agencies that required me to carry worker's compensation. I had a client in the cleaners business go out of business because of confusing, inconsistently interrupted EPA laws on the disposal of chemical solutions. I had a banking client that wasn't allowed to buy a weaker bank because of antiquated FDIC regulations. I had the SBA promise a contract, then take it back because of political favoritism in Washington.

Having said that, I received several million dollars in contracts because the federal government ramped up pressure on large corporations to find a way to do business with women, minorities and small business entities. Back then, in the oil and gas industry, where the good-ole-boy network ruled with an iron fist, only federal intervention had the power to overrule traditional patterns of exclusion. From my perspective, the federal government was the knight in shining armor, coming in to shake a few apples from the tree. However, from the perspective of product and ser-vice procurement officers sitting inside the corporations, being told to ignore established operating efficiencies, carve out chunks of their business, find qualified women and minority companies to provide services at a higher cost with increased risk of non-deliv-ery, and send a time-consuming report to Washington each quarter, not to mention the threat from opportunistic lawyers, waiting in the wings to litigate the slightest discriminatory misstep, federal intervention was a pain in the rear.

Nevertheless, over a sustained period of time, weathering inflation, stagnation and cyclical peaks and valleys, that interven-tion produced a more robust economy, seeded millions of "value-creating" small businesses that bolstered employment, fondled investment into the dark pools of society's untapped human resources and ushered in a new era of consumer spending and middle class expansion.

What's my point?

My point is I lived through that era, roughly from 1969 to 1994. I saw with my own eyes the indispensable, liberating fruits of *pain-in-the-rear* government intervention. And yet, throughout that period, there was a constant clamor for government to stay out of the business arena entirely and (during the Reagan years) to stop infringing upon our personal freedoms guaranteed by the Constitution ... code for "the right to do business or not do business with whomever I please". These opposing voices, mostly from the conservative right, felt that government programs were highly inefficient and that quotas and set-asides served as a disincentive for creating real jobs and the noble goal of allowing disenfranchised individuals to pull themselves up by their own bootstraps the old fashion way. Government needed to leave commerce alone and let the markets decide who prospered and who failed.

Now, here's the irony. Back in 1971, led by President Nixon and fiscal conservative Senator John Tower of Texas, a feverish lobbying campaign was unleashed on members of Congress to pass a massive government bailout for Lockheed Aircraft Corp, at that time the largest defense contractor in the nation.

The company contented it had been victimized by bad luck after pouring $900 million into the new TriStar Superjet. Congress passed the Emergency Loan Guarantee Act, clearing the way for $250 million (about $1.4 billion in 2009 dollars) in loan guarantees. Lockheed ended up paying the U.S. Treasury some $112 million in fees and saving over 60,000 jobs.

Again in 1975, fiscal conservatives and business executives who preached limited government and hands-off policies, rallied behind the beleaguered Chrysler Group in Detroit. A combination of high oil prices, high interest rates, bad strategies and poor sales forecasting had left the automaker and its fleet of unattractive gas-guzzlers teetering on the verge of bankruptcy and in need of a massive government bailout. With 360,000 jobs and $800 million in unfunded pension obligations hanging in the balance, Congress and the White House, under President Jimmy Carter, agreed to a $1.5 billion loan to keep the company afloat.

In 1989, at the behest of financial executives who found themselves in dire straits over huge losses in the savings and loan industry, President George H. W. Bush and both houses of Congress agreed to a taxpayer-financed bailout measure known as the Financial Institutions Reform, Recovery, and Enforcement Act (FIRREA). The act provided $50 billion to close insolvent S&Ls, established the Resolution Trust Corporation (RTC), and impose new operating constraints on the industry.

Finally, in 2008, came the Mother of all bailouts. With most of the financial systems on lockdown behind Wall Street's irresponsible purchase of toxic subprime mortgage securities and credit derivatives, President George W. Bush was forced to make an agonizing choice between the well-being of the country and the preservation of his personal legacy as a fiscal conservative. With the real prospect ... no, straight-up inevitability ... that the entire globe was about to plunge into a bottomless depression, one that would make the Great Depression of 1929 look like a walk in the park, President George Bush, Treasury Secretary Henry Paulson, and the Congress enacted the Emergency Economic Stabilization Act of 2008, a $700 billion bailout to rescue Wall Street, Main Street and the rest of the world.

The boldness and expediency of the action backed the nation and the world away from a steep cliff over which we could not afford to fall. And yet, if you listen closely to the business gurus and political pundits that dominate the airways, the debate over government's meddlesome interference in the marketplace rages on.

By now you should be seeing a pattern. But let me spell it out just in case.

Let's say your teenage daughter comes to you and asks to borrow the car and some spending money for gas and other necessities. When you asked her where she's going, she begins ranting about her rights as a teenager and your continued attempts to *get off into her business*. Why don't you trust her like other parents do? Why don't you realize she has grown up and can take care of herself?

Before she leaves, you hear her on the phone orchestrating a convincing propaganda campaign with her friends about your intrusive nature and lack of respect for her privacy. If you would just back off and allow the natural order of maturity and individual development to take place, everything would work out fine.

Then, a few hours later she calls you. She's been picked up for speeding and having alcohol in the car and needs you to get her out of jail.

The fiscal conservatives proclaim the need for government to *stay out of their business*, that is, unless they need to get out of jail. At that point of crisis, we are told government intervention is a nasty pill we'll all have to temporarily swallow.

Meanwhile, at the other end of the spectrum, proponents of proactive government are screaming for a toll booth at every entrance to the marketplace. They're saying, *"See what happens when government looks the other way?"*

They both are right in that government needs to bow into some areas and bow out of others, and trying to figure out which is a whole other book. The point is government can't completely go away and shouldn't go away. It's not an either/or proposition.

In 2008, Alan Greenspan, famously acknowledged a *flaw* in his free-market beliefs: *"I made a mistake in presuming that the self-interest of organizations, specifically banks and others, were such that they were best capable of protecting their own share-holders and their equity in the firms."*

Stated another way by Anthony Hubbard of the New Zealand *Sunday Star Times*: *"The global financial crisis showed that cold and calculating money men can go crazy. Sober bankers lose their marbles. The hallowed theory that the invisible hand of the market would produce profit, and plenty for all, was shown to be nonsense. Business could cut its own throat".*

As a young entrepreneur and king/queen of your mound, this historical perspective is critical to your decision-making, especially when it comes to this particular key performance variable. Noble-minded business peers will tell you to avoid the "government trap". Don't do business with the government. Don't allow your operational strategies to get tied up with or dependent upon what the government is doing.

To this naive advice I have one word: Hogwash. If government policies open up an opportunistic door for you to walk though, don't walk ... run. This is what the big military contractors do all the time. They realize, as the pendulum of political influence swings from one side to the other, there is a very good chance the opportunity will soon disappear. So companies like Blackwater USA (Xe Services) pounce on it right away.

The 2009 Economic Stimulus Package designated $8 billion to perform home weatherization inspections and home weather-ization improvements. The Department of Energy recently handed out $47 million to fund eight research and development projects to support the production of bio-fuels, bio-energy, and high-value bio-based products. The American Recovery and Reinvestment Act provided $40 billion for energy and renewable energy programs. Do you know anything about windmills? How fast can you learn?

<u>As a young small business owner, bombarded by high-minded, patriotic-sounding rhetoric, you need to be able to see through the fog of hypocrisy</u>. The same Reaganites that cry out for the right to do business (or not do business) with whomever they please, are the same executives pressuring the State Department and Commerce Department to force China to open up its markets to American companies. These Constitutional advocates of

personal freedom are saying, "The Chinese good-ole-boy network has locked us out. It's not fair. Why should they be able to do business with ... whomever they please?"

Forget the ideological and political wrangling. For the sake of your business stay focused on the prize. Government intervention can be a good thing. Just make sure the pendulum swings to your side of the table.

Back to the AUME diagram.

Reasonable learning curve for existing personnel

Again, in this category, Option #1 failed miserably. The raw score of 1 reflected the team's sentiment that cloud computing was a Bill Gates thing. Some team members were still having trouble mastering ground computer, much less entering the Cloud. The consensus pointed to an opportunity that existing team competencies did not allow Averest to pursue.

Ample outside resources and vendors

Option #1 received a 99 in this category, and rightly so. In some markets, large suppliers such as Microsoft, or retailers such as Wal-Mart have the potential to dictate the future success of your product or service. Think about it. In the early 1990's, if you were a computer maker and Microsoft didn't allow you to buy Windows at the pre-installed wholesale price, how could you compete?

Fortunately, cloud computing offers an expanded array of suppliers, including server manufacturers, software providers and security configurations. But these resources mean nothing if Averest can't muster the capital to get into the market. And so we move on.

Current operation adds to competitive advantage

Again, in this category, Option #1 received a failing score. There was little about the current operation that enhanced Averest's chances of successfully competing in the Cloud. In comparison, Option #5: Diamond Tools sale and distribution received a raw score of 80. You already have a warehouse, delivery trucks, a driver and sales personnel. You're located in Texas, a state that many national construction companies call home. And with the state's massive highway and bridge systems, there's a very high probability some of the federal infrastructure money will be spent in close proximity to you.

The cloud option didn't offer these advantages. Essentially, you'd be starting from scratch. So long, Cloud.

When you look at the total weighted score of 3532 for Option #1, compared to the winning score of 6294 for Option #11, you understand why. Option #1 is a poor fit for your organization. You want to make sure high-tech worker Bradford sees what you see and then move on.

Now that you've gotten the hang of it, let's explore the pros and cons of other options. Since Option #8: Electric Batteries for Hybrid Vehicles earned some reasonably high scores, let's take a closer look under the hood to determine why it wasn't chosen by the Averest team as the final option.

OPTION #8

Electric Batteries for Hybrid Vehicles

In an effort to curb greenhouse gas emissions from conventional internal combustion automobile engines and reduce America's overall dependency on foreign energy sources, the Obama administration has pledged $2.4 billion in federal grants to develop next-generation electric vehicles and batteries, and bring one million plug-in hybrids to American roads by 2015. This commitment has opened up a huge market related to the production, distribution and recycling of lithium ion batteries, and construction of alternative fueling stations that dispense E85 fuel, electricity and natural gas.

Most experts agree the market will be expanding for at least a decade, perhaps even longer as newly discovered technologies drive experimentation and alternative approaches to fuel efficiency. And yet, your team has turned down this option as a potential fit for Averest. Let's review each key performance variable to find out why.

Key
Performance
Variable **Matches existing organizational core values**

Option #8 received a raw score of 88 in this all-important category; a very respectable score but lower than Option #10's high score of 95. The primary reason for Option #8's reduced score was embedded in the uncertainty over current disposal methods for the lithium batteries and the ultimate impact it might have on the environment. Larvae Daily pointed out that toxic chemicals such as hexfluorophosphate had the potential to pollute the earth, a process in which Averest shouldn't be involved.

Though experts disagreed on the potential ecological threat posed by disposal, they all agreed that mining the lithium from the ground had built-in processes that were traditionally harmful to the environment. The 88 score was somewhat of a compromise between acknowledging potential harm and not knowing for sure.

Key
Performance
Variable

Manageable initial cost to enter the market

In this category, Option #8 received a raw score of 60, ten points above neutral. The score represented a strategic approach driven by synthetical thinking and not easy to discern with the naked eye.

The construction of most of the current lithium factories carried a hefty price tag into the millions of dollars. The team's research pointed to South Korean electronics giant LG which had just finished the world's largest lithium-ion plant for electric vehicle traction batteries for just under a billion. With the help of a $249 million grant from the U.S. Department of Energy, A123 Systems had built a multi-million dollar plant in Livonia, Michigan, the largest in North America.

The good news was that in recent months, new technology had emerged to allow a scaled-down manufacturing model to be built for just under $50 million. With grant money, set aside guarantees, aggressive bank financing and a local energy partner or two, the team felt they had a shot at pulling it off. They rated the possibility slightly better than neutral, thus the raw score of 60.

Attractive return on investment/Profit margins

With no dominate supplier in the market, a lack of combustion engine alternatives besides hybrid, and growing global demand, the team confirmed analysts' predictions of an expanding lithium-ion battery market set to exceed $12 billion by 2020.

In this category, Option #8, with a raw score of 70, was passing, but barely. The dynamics of a long-shot investment scenario involving banks and undetermined partners to build a $50 million mini-manufacturing model contributed to the low score. The reasoning was based on several assumptions.

If the necessary investments materialized and Averest succeeded in building the mini model, the economies of scale would be substantially lower compared to the larger plants in Japan and Michigan. Since operating profits for the industry currently ranged from 17% to 30%, Averest could expect to earn profits at the lower end of the spectrum, perhaps 12% to 14%, In other words, the market would be growing, large competitors would continue to find economies of scale in their production processes, and prices would begin to fall. By earning profit margins at the lower end, Averest would not be able to match falling prices or be competitive on price, alone.

Nevertheless, because of the guaranteed government-mandated *"set aside"* purchases from small businesses, this scenario would not prevent Averest from entering the market and making money. Automakers would still have to buy a small percentage of their batteries from Averest and other small and women-owned businesses at a government-subsidized higher price. This temporary grace period might allow the Averest team, operating under the aggressive Anthead System, to discover other opportunities in the industry, including recharging stations and safe disposal techniques. The score of 70 represented a vote of conservative optimism.

High level of team interest/buy-in

In this category, Option #8 received an impressive raw score of 90. Team members were excited about the opportunity to tackle a bold concept and felt that existing organizational competencies were a match to the battery assembly and distribution challenges that lay ahead.

One of the advantages of entering a rapidly evolving market with a limited number of seasoned experts working for the competition was the existence of a level playing field where everyone would be scrambling to innovate and create value. Beyond that, the team felt a sense of fulfillment in ushering in alternative green technology that reduced the nation's dependence on foreign oil.

Ease of exit when market plays out

Not unexpectedly, in this category Option #8 also received a failing grade of 40. Manufacturing plants, large or small, require heavy investments in infrastructure. An offspring of the machine bureaucracy with emphasis on standardizing all tasks and maintaining specific systems that must adhere to explicit levels of quality control, there is really no way around it.

Critical to the production of lithium-ion batteries are certain complex high-energy processes including chemical oxidation, organic solvent transformation, metal striping and laser-welding, to name a few. Certain pre-packaged modules reduce the need to start from scratch on all aspects of production. But the bottom line is a heavy investment by Averest in specialized equipment and expertise is unavoidable. Getting out of the market would be painful.

Able to compete and protect/Barriers

As mentioned earlier, this is an extremely important category. And yet, Option #8 received a low score of 10. The 10 injected a dose of realism into the business model that allowed Averest to enter the market and make money through set-asides, and yet not be able to compete effectively against larger competitors that could create economies of scale.

With business legend GE as the largest cash investor, as well as existing contracts with Navistar Inc. and Chrysler, A123 Systems has opened the largest lithium ion automotive battery production facility in North America. Mitsubishi Motors Corp. and South Korea-based LG Chem have entered a joint venture to develop an advanced automotive lithium-ion battery system based on superior long-life technology. Toyota Motor Corp has entered a joint venture with Matsushita Electric Industrial Co and started full-scale production of lithium-ion batteries for its gasoline-electric hybrids. These serious moves toward long-term vertical integration indicate a strong commitment by major players to compete for years to come. Without the government set asides, Averest would have a difficult time surviving. Both barriers to entry and formable alliances among competitors signal a need to explore other market options.

Opportunity to differentiate/Add Bells & Whistles

Option #8 received a failing grade of 40 in this category. The SAE International's Battery Standards Committee has developed benchmark safety performance standards for lithium-ion battery systems with more stringent standards for cells, modules, packs, and ancillary subsystems systems on the way. This means manufacturers are limited in how the end product can perform, or fail to perform, in critical areas such as discharge pulse power, regenerative pulse power, available energy, efficiency, cycle life, system weight, system volume, and self discharge. This is similar to natural gas shut-off valves and utility meters. The voltage in a hybrid vehicle could kill a perspective customer. There is no room for error in the minimum performance required.

Having said that, ever-evolving technologies related to the use of lighter materials, different metal combinations and more efficient chemical reactions inside cells allow each manufacturer to pursue innovation and differentiation at the R&D level. In other words, you have the liberty to use a typewriter, laptop, tablet or Smartphone; just so that twenty-page report is turned in by noon tomorrow.

The problem with Averest is it has no R&D functionality. With the business model your team has envisioned, you will be assembling pre-packed modules and selling them as a single battery unit. At the assembly level, there is very little room for differentiation.

Government intervention in our favor

In this category, Option #8 received a maximum score of 99. From your perspective, government intervention is a beautiful thing, perhaps, not enough to pay out AIG type retention bonuses to your staff, but certainly a game-changer in the way of facilitating your entry into the market.

As mentioned earlier, the government has committed $2.4 billion in federal grants to develop next-generation electric vehicles and batteries. They have also set aside a designated portion exclusively for small business to participate in the process. Finally, to encourage end users to purchase plug-in hybrid electric car, they have underwritten a one-time $7,500 tax credit for each purchase.

For the purpose of comparison, if we look at Option #9: Energy Conservation, we see it also garnered an impressive score of 99. The government's 2009 Economic Stimulus Package designated more than $8 billion for weatherization inspections and home weatherization improvements (seal cracks, gaps, and holes around doors, windows, and pipes) including the special Weather-ization Assistance Program (WAP) to assist low-income families who lacked resources to invest in energy efficiency.

In both instances, the government is doing its share to provide small business opportunities, while addressing a specific need in society. With both options, government intervention is on your side.

Conversely, Option #6, Green Haul and Clean up of petrochemical spills, received a raw score of 1. Government is extremely demanding when it comes to adherence to disposal and dumping procedures. You can go out and clean up a toxic spill. But once the stuff is in your tanker truck, where do you take it? And how many tracking reports will you have to fill out to submit to governmental agencies verifying your actions. In this category, the pendulum swings in the opposite direction. Government will beat you into the ground.

Reasonable learning curve for existing personnel

In this category, Option #8 received a raw score of 70, reflecting the team's mixed sentiment that a process so labor-intense, with critical government-mandated standardization and specialized expertise might pose a major challenge to existing team members, especially Riley and the other two techs in the warehouse. The team felt ultimately, everyone would master their individual contributions. But the learning process was going to take some time.

Ample outside resources and vendors

Option #8 received a neutral score of 50 in this category, partly because of conflicting expert projections and partly because of the volatility still found in the marketplace.

Lithium, along with cobalt, nickel, and manganeseis are key ingredients used in the production of lithium-ion batteries. A few financial experts had speculated that as more factories ramped up at breakneck speed, there could be a worldwide lithium shortage. This proved to be a false assumption (unclean or corrupt data).

First, lithium is not rare. It's as common as lead and reasonably simple to extract from the ground. Secondly, lithium-ion batteries don't really use that much lithium. Only about a thirtieth of the cost of producing the battery can be linked to lithium, compared to cobalt which represents more than half the total production cost. Cobalt is used in hybrid electric vehicles, solar energy panels, cell phones, pagers and laptops and is considered a strategic metal by the U.S. government. And yet, there is not a single cobalt mine in the United States. The nation seemed poised to go from dependency on foreign oil to dependency on foreign cobalt. In the team's analysis, this was the point of potential volatility. But no one could really say for sure.

Key Performance Variable

Current operation adds to competitive advantage

In this category, Option #8 squeezed out a passing grade of 70.

Averest already has a plastics plant/warehouse that is large enough to be converted into a module assembly operation for lithium-ion battery parts coming in from different vendors. You have delivery vehicles and a driver that are already built into the cost structure. You have salespersons and administrators to support the operation. What you don't have (and this is critical) is the technical expertise to move the product from the concept stage to reality.

This would be an excellent time to examine a competing option with similar challenges. Let's take a brief look at Option #3: Parent Outsourcing, where the existing warehouse means nothing.

According to IBIS World, a Los Angeles research company, parents electing to outsource their child-related duties such as child care, coaching and tutoring has become a $56 billion industry. There are some ninety-three million children out there under the age of twenty-one, requiring some form of support and/or intervention and preparation in order to meet public and private goals essential to their development as productive citizens.

Retail child care centers account for 41% of the market, closely followed by nanny and babysitting services with a 30% market share. The remaining 29% is split between sports coaching, exam preparation and tutoring, educational consultants and mentoring specialists such as those that break children of thumb-sucking and wetting to bed.

At first glance, one might think a team of counselors, educators and coaches with advanced degrees and certificates would be required to enter this business. It would be the same as saying only doctors and nurses could enter the hospital industry. In fact, the team found that success in the Parent Outsourcing industry, especially in the child care segment, hinged on being able to acquire the mandatory local and state licenses and permits, and hiring a competent support staff to perform the requested tasks.

The same holds true for Option #8. You're going to have to hire the lithium-ion battery production experts you need, while paying for additional training for your three plastics techs. Since you're happy with your current team and have elected not to lay anyone off, this is your most feasible solution. The raw score of 70 in this category represents these important steps. Just know it's going to take some time for the transformation to evolve.

Finally, the moment for which we've been waiting.

How did Option #11 manage to earn a total weighted score higher than all the others? Let's stick with our previous procedure and walk through each key performance variable in the AUME Matrix to determine exactly how our future ended up, happily, on the toilet.

OPTION #11

Production and distribution of custom toilets

Around 1596, England's Sir John Harrington invented a crude water-operated "water closet", the forerunner to the modern flushing toilet. Before then, residents of Medieval Europe emptied indoor chamber pots directly into the streets. By the time London's modern sewer system was completed in 1853, several inventors had created a pan with a sliding door that allowed users to pull a fresh water lever to wash contents into a public drain. This marked the yucky but humble beginnings of the modern toilet manufacturing industry.

In recent decades, Japanese toilet makers such as Toto and INAX Corp. have dominated the world of bathroom hygiene with an array of gadgets, including posterior shower jets, tantalizing perfume bursts, germ-resistant seats, noise-masking audio and NoMix receptacles that collect urine separately from feces, instead of mixing it together.

If you're feeling a bit squeamish, pull yourself together! This industry is generating $7 billion a year. The United States, China, Japan, Germany, and Italy account for 62 % of the market with upwardly mobile middle classes in India, Brazil and Russia buying at double digit rates.

Several factors have contributed to the market's unparalleled growth and innovation. Perennial worldwide droughts and polluted water sources have created an escalating water shortage. Frost & Sullivan's Water Management Services (DSD) estimates since 1999, global freshwater resources have declined by 4.2%, annually. Secondly, older toilets made before the 1980s, using about 3 gallons per flush, are being replaced by high efficiency toilets (HETs) that use 1.28 gallons or less. Thirdly, an aging population of Baby Boomers with an emphasis on health-consciousness is replacing its existing toilets with highly complex, computerized "Intelligent Toilets" that provide urine analysis, blood pressure and body temperature readings, while also measuring the user's weight via an inbuilt floor scale.

Finally, sales are being driven by prestige buying. Although a durable selection of toilets is available in the $20 to $50 range, many Chinese consumers are spending upward of $3,000 for new luxury models to flaunt their new-found wealth. These compensatory purchases account for over 5% of the total toilet market share.

Your team has chosen this option over the other potential selections for many reasons. As always we will review each key performance variable in the AUME Matrix to see why.

Key
Performance
Variable

Matches existing organizational core values

Option #11 received a raw score of 88 in this all-important category; a very respectable score but lower than Option #9's high score of 95. The primary reason for Option #11's less than perfect rating had to do with its perceived lackluster potential to make team member feel they could wow customers while experiencing a strong sense of accomplishment, reinforcing their belief that what they did really mattered.

From a psychological perspective, *"toilet talk"* is off-limits. A survey conducted by AGP revealed 57% of respondents felt embarrassed when discussing toilet matter, 40% didn't want to communicate with anyone while using the toilet and 26%, some with functional disorders, didn't want to use a public restroom at all.

Now imagine your business team electing to enter the toilet market where members would be expected to discuss these embarrassing issues all day long.

The saving grace for this category ultimately rested on Averest's specific business model which pursued a medical niche tied to the development of superior, custom-made "Intelligent Toilets" for the elderly, medically disabled and home-bound Baby Boomers. The team found virtue in this narrowly focused market stream and felt it would be worth coming to work each day to improve the standard of life for an underserved segment of the population. Examining subsequent key performance variables, we will have the opportunity to discuss this niche in detail.

Key Performance Variable

Manageable initial cost to enter the market

In this category, Option #11 received a raw score of 95. The high score represented the team's belief that many of the elements necessary to transition into the marketplace were already in place.

Consider the raw materials that make up most toilets. Polystyrene is a liquid hydrocarbon made from petroleum and is one of the most widely available plastics used in the toilet manufacturing process. (Did I say plastic?) For wooden toilet seat, which you don't anticipate using in your high-end, "custom-made" strategy, maple or birch chips would be used in a blend with an easily obtainable plastic resin called melamine. Finally, readily available stainless steel and copper base metals, in conjunction with a special vitreous china clay, would be used for tank fixtures; the entire apparatus held together by sturdy plastic joints.

Did I say plastic again?

Averest is already in the plastics business. Riley and the other techs are well-versed in the use of polystyrene in the production of its CD's, DVD's and tool boxes. Neither wood chips nor melamine nor any of the other necessary ingredients in the production process pose an insurmountable financial challenge. Beyond that, the actual heating and molding process is considered a low tech, moderately expensed, affordable operation.

The major costs would stem from the purchase of computerized lifts, water flow and measuring components and the expertise to assemble all the parts into a working unit. The team felt, with minimal bank financing and available government EPA grants, as well as private medical grants, the transformation of the warehouse, tech training and establishment of distribution channels would be quite feasible.

Key Performance Variable **Attractive return on investment/Profit margins**

In 2010, the $7 billion sanitaryware market was estimated to be growing at a steady rate of 8% to 10%, annually. Among major segments such as toilet-bidets (toilets with nozzles that wash the anus and genitals) the growth rate climbed to 13%. The markup for major producers such as American Standard, Kohler and Toto averages about 25%.

In this category, Option #11 received a raw score of 90. The prospect for sustained profits remained rosy for several reasons. Besides previously mentioned drivers such as the global water shortage and technological obsolescence, cultural influences from India, China and Japan seem to be moving US consumers to view washlets, bidets and paperless bowel procedures with greater acceptance. Similar to acupuncture, Zen meditation and other Oriental healing and health food crazes that invaded the US market in the late 1980's, the research showed that new toilet protocol was laying the groundwork for a quiet revolution in domestic sanitary-ware purchases.

Key Performance Variable

High level of team interest/buy-in

In this category, Option #11 received a raw score of 70. The rating wasn't as bad as the 15 Option #7: Prisoner Transport received. However, the low score certainly signaled a collective revulsion to the toilet business, lingering beneath the surface.

This is where your skills as a visionary come into play. Until success takes root, it will be your job to reinforce the logic, virtue and potential of the choice your team has made. Think about the lives that were lost in WW II, or more recently, Iraq and Afghanistan. Someone had to constantly remind the troops their efforts were worthwhile. Though choosing a market with a stigma attached is far less profound, the need to encourage the team and keep a positive spin on their daily contributions is equally important.

There is a direct correlation between motivation and performance. Famous humanistic psychologist Abraham Maslow based performance on satisfying a specific hierarchy of needs ... from basic survival needs for food, water and air to high-level, self-actualizing needs such as self-aware, self-image and personal growth. In every organization, an assortment of individual passion, energy, and predispositions are thrown into a big pot, stirred up, and in the end, a specific taste emerges. That taste can be exceedingly sour if personal biases based on unsatisfied needs prevent team members from being fully committed or involved.

Not everyone can work for an AIDS clinic or gambling casino or CIA black ops killing team. The SEC employees that turned a deaf ear to warnings about Bernie Madoff's $50 billion Ponzi scheme were not necessarily incompetent. Rather, they were uninspired, or some would say, alternately inspired. In 2004, SEC Attorney Genevievette Walker-Lightfoot in Compliance Inspections and Examinations found numerous inconsistencies in Madoff's operation. After reporting this information to her supervisor's branch chief, she was told to move on to other investigations.

In a pro-business culture, heavily influenced by upper management complicity and top-down pressure to avoid becoming a cog in the wheel, Attorney Walker-Lightfoot had a lower level need for survival, that is, a need to follow orders and keep her job. These intrinsic influences do not simply go away. They lurk in the background either preventing or inspiring team member to operate with maximum efficiency.

Here's the uncut, vomit-on-the-floor bottom-line. Although Option #11 was the winner, you cannot ignore the raw score of 70 in this important category. There is an unmet need lurking in the background; the need to feel good (proud) about one's line of work. You can certainly overcome this obstacle, however, with a visionary emphasis on the valuable benefits your operation will bring to the market and society as a whole. Somewhere out there an elderly or disabled person will be singing your praises for making their life more simple and enjoyable. But this is a song you need to sing to your team members first.

As a leader and visionary, you need to make them see what you see and feel proud to be a part of this "extraordinary process" that allows your team, with all its unique competencies, to deliver a revolutionary product never before seen in the marketplace. Never downplay the importance of what you do. Each day, take time out to extol the benefits of satisfying a need that is critical to the customers you serve. Inspire team members to perform at their highest level of efficiency, uninhibited by old fogy stigmas that don't mean a hill of beans.

Key Performance Variable

Ease of exit when market plays out

In this category, Option #11 received an impressive score of 93. The manufacturing infrastructure necessary to process the raw materials such as polystyrene, gypsum plaster, vitreous china clay, stainless steel base metals, etc. and then assemble them into a computerized, mechanized shippable unit would not require a deep investment in vertical integration. Similar to Dell's Just-in-time inventory system which orders parts based on meeting existing customer orders, Averest would employ an ordering system that minimized shelf inventory.

If the market played out, one of the most costly components with which to dispose would be the large ovens used to bake the toilets into a hard, durable finish. Beyond that, the transition to another promising market should be relatively painless.

Able to compete and protect/Barriers

In this extremely important category, Option #11 received another dubious score of 70. Let's take a closer look at the proposed business model to determine why.

In the Appreciative Inquiry Dream state, the team envisioned the production and distribution of custom-made toilets specifically targeting the elderly, disabled and convenience-oriented Baby Boomer markets. The production process would include the conversion of easily obtainable raw materials into a partially finished generic toilet. The toilet would be customized with computerized medical equipment and Asian-style conveniences such as noise-masking DVD players, vertical lifts and suspension pulleys and bidet water jets capable of watching the users anus and genitals parts.

From a competitive standpoint, the team felt Averest maintained a strategic advantage in several areas. Being located in the Houston metroplex, in close proximity to petroleum refineries which produced polystyrene and other raw materials needed in the production process, Averest's shipping costs would be significantly reduced, compared to competitors requiring the same raw materials a thousand miles away. Secondly, with Averest in close proximity to the internationally famous Texas Medical Center, many cutting-edge technological advances for the elderly and disabled would be more accessible from the standpoint of testing and experimentation. Medical research facilities desiring to test health-related technology would feel comfortable using Averest as a local guinea pig, and then ultimately partnering with the Averest (medical) brand to provide physically challenged patients with new and improved solutions, contributing to their effort to live a normal life.

Beyond that, the local positioning would give Averest an opportunity to go after its own medical grant funding for experimentation into more effective methods of addressing current and future disabilities.

Local firms such as Medical Robotics LLC received $25,000 in grants to perfect a robotic catheter insertion device. A local consortium of Houston-based medical research institutions received $33.6 million to study the diagnosis and treatment of traumatic brain injuries. Three Texas Medical Center institutions received more than $100 million from the National Institutes of Health to tackle cancer, heart disease and autism. Finally, the 2009 Recovery Act included $200 million in grant funding for medical device innovation.

Everyone felt that Averest could definitely compete. The low score of 70 reflected the answer to the question of how long. With dominate players such as Toto, American Standard and Kohler already in the marketplace, how long would it take them to copycat Averest's most popular medical models and then use their economies of scale to sell the same product at half the cost?

The traditional protective barriers would involve filing legal patents. But getting the government to grant a patent takes years. Another strategy would be to form exclusive strategic relationships with local medical providers that currently serve the elderly and disabilities market. But such an agreement would require paying a royalty or sharing profits with perspective partners. The question would then center on whether the operation could sustain margins large enough to pay partners and still offer a competitive price in the marketplace.

Another unexpected consideration was the effect of Japan's earthquake-tsunami on Toto's ability to produce and deliver toilets worldwide. With plants in Morrow, Georgia as well as Ciénega de Flores and Monterrey, Mexico the prospect of a slowdown seemed remote. However, the ongoing scandal about Toto's blazing-bidets (washlets that overheat and catch on fire) had reduced Tito's dominate 63% bidet global market share, and perhaps, opened a door of vulnerability that worked in Averest's favor.

The team was optimistic. However, the 70 reflected the unpredictability involved in an option selection that, considering the lack of protective barriers, seemed to be a very good choice.

Opportunity to differentiate/Add Bells & Whistles

This was an easy one. Option #11 received a stellar grade of 99. The team was excited to discover toilets could be made in all sizes and shapes and equipped with an endless array of bells and whistles.

Pursuing a high-end medical niche, Averest would offer exceeding comfort and flexibility for those customers needing to adjust the unit's height and angle, perform medical monitoring and difficult hygiene functions, and avoid common discomforts such as the "cold seat" syndrome. In addition, Averest would offer customers Maria's exclusive line of toiletries, scented toilet paper and meditation CD's to "set the mood" and transform an age-old human necessity into a more rewarding experience.

Government intervention in our favor

In this category, Option #11 received an impressive rating of 90. Although the aggressive legislation associated with solar, wind and hybrid vehicles was not apparent with toilets, there were many federal grants supporting medical device research in the industry as well as legislation at the state level that emphasized water conservation. The team found that Former California Gov. Arnold Schwarzenegger had signed a bill mandating 50% of toilets offered for sale in 2010 meet the high-efficiency standards, ramping up to 100% by 2014. The U.S. Environmental Protection Agency had also drawn a line in the sand with its coveted "WaterSense" label, requiring new units be able to flush using a maximum flush volume of 1.28 gallons and have the ability to remove a minimum of 350 grams of solid waste per flush. According to the EPA, WaterSense toilets save 4,000 gallons of water per person annually.

The team couldn't find any small business government set asides. However, with so many other factors contributing to the growth of the market, the absence of set asides did not represent a major deterrent, at least, not until the point when the larger manufacturers started to copycat and price cut.

Key Performance Variable

Reasonable learning curve for existing personnel

In this category, Option #11 received another favorable raw score of 90. As we mentioned earlier, unlike cloud computing or firing up a nuclear plant, toilet manufacturing is basically low tech. Riley and the other techs were already familiar with plastics, molding and the assembly process. Sales personnel were accustomed to selling plastic components. With the increased commissions on big ticket items, there was no doubt they would leap into the new, exotic line of inventory with both feet. Secretary/receptionist Maria had shown a natural interest in aging products. This would serve as a springboard for her transformation into managing the line of toiletries and scented papers.

You'll have to invest in a new hire, perhaps, a foreman or general manager that has worked for Toto or Kohler, and is looking for a greater opportunity. This will be tricky because the Anthead System requires more than just a person with factory knowledge. You'll want someone that can morph and grow and be open, perhaps, to stock options to reduce the high upfront salary. Like Apple when it originally started, your resourcefulness in recruiting should not be limited to the money you have in the bank.

Learning new processes will be an ongoing thing at Averest. So get use to it. As we said earlier, success will depend heavily on your ability to know each member of your team and how their individual competencies fit in a new market assault. Option #11 provides a reasonable platform for extending the team's learning capabilities toward a successful end.

Key Performance Variable **Ample outside resources and vendors**

Option #11 received another favorable raw score of 90. The raw material, equipment and expertise were readily available for anyone wanting to enter the market. This fact lowered the score associated with barriers to keep competitors out of the market. But these same conditions made it simple for Averest to get in. If only you could just close the door behind you. Perhaps, with the right marketing strategies that discourage others from wanting to try, you can, at least, narrow the crack.

Key Performance Variable

Current operation adds to competitive advantage

In this category, Option #11 received another stellar score of 99.

Averest already has a plastics plant/warehouse large enough to be converted into an assembly operation for custom-made toilets. The personnel are already in place. The company's location on the outskirts of Houston gives it access to petroleum factories and medical facilities that will play an intricate part in the success of the operation. Even the nearby Port of Houston will come into play as Averest eventually reaches out to growth markets in Turkey, Romania, India and Brazil.

Beyond that, research showed traditionally dry states with chronic water shortages such as Texas, Arizona and California were experiencing a disproportionate increase in sales of dual-flush, water-efficient models that saved millions each year on water usage. Each of these markets was in geographic striking distance and offered an opportunity to expand sales beyond the local medical niche.

Let's briefly revisit the top section of the AUME Matrix and then we're done.

The Ant Contribution (Anticipated Contribution) row flows out of a worksheet similar to the one shown earlier on page 214.

AUME Sample Feed

I say similar because it doesn't have to look exactly like this one. The objective is to capture the potential contributions of each team member to see if there are signs of overlap or a hole that needs to be filled. Soldier/accountant Prewett is resigning so you already know you're going to need a new accountant with additional expertise. Also, pursuing Option #11, you're going to have to hire a technician thoroughly familiar with the new manufacturing process. Finally, if Driver Ortega doesn't get his act together, you're going to have to hire a driver, maybe two.

But there's something else missing from this scenario, something that both the worksheet and the AUME Matrix have failed to capture, and rightly so. This information is intended for *your eyes only*, or maybe I should say, for *your brain only*.

Your organization is made up of people; frail humans whose lives can change or even vanish, regrettably, in the blink of an eye. What's not on the worksheet is your personal strategy to deal with the normal attrition that accompanies any business. Companies such as Microsoft, Marriott and IBM refer to it as a succession plan ... identifying candidates with the potential to assume greater responsibility in the organization; and then providing critical exposure and development that facilitates their move into these key roles.

Inside the Anthead System, however, because functions are so intertwined, the replacement process is so much more important. Thus, it becomes necessary to craft a replacement strategy that anticipates internal personnel adjustments necessary to keep your operation afloat.

If Drone Howard gets hit by a bus or accepts a more attractive position with another company, whom, in the organization, will take his place? If you don't know right now, it's okay. But it won't be okay in the future when your operation is grinding on all cylinders. You need to start thinking about these unwanted scenarios and preparing a strategy to address them.

One strategy is cross training.

Let's say you decide High-tech worker Bradford is the logical person to take Drone Howard's place. That means you should begin to expose High-tech worker Bradford to portions of Drone Howard's job. Certain assignments should be shared (in an unobtrusive way), allowing High-tech worker Bradford to perform similar duties. The same holds true for Secretary/receptionist Maria who might be able to step in for Scout/salesperson Sally.

Now you see why this information is for your eyes only. Employees tend to get the jitters when there's any talk of their replacement. There's a perceived violation of the psychological contract that protects their value inside the organization. The worksheet should never reflect this synthetical process. But you should always be aware of the critical impact it has on each team member's responsibilities.

One last detour and then we're finished.

All along, we've been exploring the benefits of using some extraordinary new processes associated with predictive analysis. You can call it analytics, data mining or enterprise decision-making. But, essentially, what we've been doing is placing bets on the future. Not unlike stock brokers or financial portfolio consultants, we've been gather intelligence about the past and present to predict future outcomes. As your organization matures, this practice will become even more prevalent, but with greater risks and rewards at stake.

Think about a startup oil and gas company drilling one small well out in the dusty Oklahoma boondocks. As the company grows, one well turns into ten wells with a higher cost of exploration, higher failure rate per well, but a greater potential for massive payoffs in the end. As you attempt to deploy resources and seize opportunities in an ever-expanding operation, predictive analysis will play a key role in your effort to keep the company solvent. Consequently, the better you become at it, the better your chances are to survive and grow.

Under the Anthead System, you'll be developing predictive analysis teams that place *bets*, and then, are rewarded for their efficiency. A few large companies like Hewlett-Packard, Goldman Sachs and Eli Lilly are already experimenting with the extraordinary concepts such as Random-Matrix Theory which uncovers hidden correlations within masses of data. However, because of traditional corporate bureaucracy, most companies have been slow to fully implement these processes.

The reasoning behind this new approach is simple: There are vast amounts of untapped information inside the "Wisdom of the Mound" that can make decision-making more reliable.

Involving people far down the corporate hierarchy to make predictions about sales and vendor behavior, Hewlett-Packard found that the predictive analysis teams beat official forecasts 75% of the time.

Here's a simple scenario. You give five people in your organization $100 each to bet on what the sales figures will look like in September, October and November. This is money in an account on the computer so it never leaves your pocket. The participants are able to buy stocks that reflect the sales figures in which they most believe. They can buy and sell stocks to each other based on their evolving perceptions of the marketplace. In the end, the person holding the most accurate stock certificates wins the "actual" $100. (At that point, it does leave your pocket.) Then the process resumes with other future sales outcomes as betting targets. Only this time, the losers start with $75 and the winner gets their $100 ($25 x 4) added to his or her new account. At some point the "broke people" who have been most ineffective in their predictions don't have any money to bet and are off the betting team.

The process can be a lot of fun. But if implemented correctly, it can also provide you with insight never imagined.

That's as much as I'm going to say about predictive analysis internal markets this time around. In future writings we will explore more advanced applications of this intriguing phenomenon capable of placing the full power of the Wisdom of the Mound at your disposal. For now, however, seek every opportunity to extract input from team members across the entire organizational spectrum. In the long run, this useful information will pay precious dividends in your quest to throttle your company's engines full steam ahead.

Well, that's it, the end of this extraordinary journey ... at least for me. I hope you have learned a few indelible truths that will carry you boldly into the future, a future filled with struggles, disappointments and setbacks, but more importantly, opportunities of a lifetime. With your new-found perspective, you should see the world a bit differently now. And hopefully, you'll take flight on the unprecedented winds of promise, soaring boldly above the clouds. Just remember the old sign on President Harry S. Truman's desk: *"The Buck Stops Here."* With the help of your incredible team, the decisions are yours to make, the future, yours to take.

Good luck, my Anthead comrades. Have a wonderful journey ahead.

THE END

BIBLIOGRAPHY

Berinato, Scott. (October 15, 2003), The state of information security 2003, Retrieved April 24, 2008, from http://www.cio.com/article/29841/The_State_of_Information_Security.

Brooks, D. (2011). The Social Animal: The Hidden Source of Love, Character, and Achievement, New York: Random House.

Buffington, J. (2009), The death of management: Restoring value to the U.S. economy, Santa Barbara, Calif: Praeger.

Chess, Wayne A., and Julia M. Norlin, (1988) Human Behavior and the Social Environment: A Social Systems Model, Boston: Allyn and Bacon, Inc.

Christensen, Clayton M. (1997). The innovator's dilemma: when new technologies cause great firms to fail. Harvard Business Press.

COMPETING ON ANALYTICS. By: Davenport, Thomas H., Harvard Business Review, 00178012, Jan2006, Vol. 84, Issue 1.

Frank , Robert J., George, Jeffery P. & Narasimhan (2006), Competitor Delivers More For Less, New Jersey Wharton School Publishing.

Google Finance, Retrieved April 27, 2007, from http://en.wikipedia.org/wiki/Weighted_average_cost_of_capital.

Hagel, J. & Brown, J.S. (2001). Your next IT strategy. Harvard Business Review. 105- 113.

Hall, D. T., & Moss, J. E. (1998). The new protean career contract: Helping organizations and employees adapt. Organizational Dynamics, 26 (3), p. 22–38.

Hammond, S.A. (1998). The thin book of appreciative inquiry (2nd ed). Plano, TX: Thin Book Publishing.

Goldberg, R.A. (2001). Implementing a professional development system through appreciative inquiry. Leadership and Organization Development Journal. Vol.22 Iss.2. Bradford: Emerald Group Publishing Ltd. pp56-61.

Help Net Security. (2007, February), The importance of IT security, Retrieved May 12, 2008, from: http://www.net-security.org/news.php?id=13532

HURDLE RATES FOR SCREENING CAPITAL EXPENDITURE PROPOSALS. By: Brigham, Eugene F.. Financial Management (1972), Autumn75, Vol. 4 Issue 3, p17-26, 10p, 7 charts, 1 graph; (*AN 5031408*).

Identification of Strategic Information Systems Opportunities: Applying and Comparing Two Methodologies, Bergeron, Francois, Buteau, Chantal, Raymond, Louis. MIS Quarterly. Minneapolis: Mar 1991. Vol. 15, Iss. 1; p. 89 (13 pages).

Johnson, B. (1998). Polarity management - A summary introduction. Middleville, MI: Polarity Management Associates.

Just-in-Time Delivery Comes to Knowledge Management: Davenport, Thomas H.; Glaser, John. Harvard Business Review, Jul2002, Vol. 80 Issue 7, p107-111, 5p, 2 color; (AN 6899237).

BIBLIOGRAPHY

Kanter, J., (2003). Ten Hot Information Technology (IT) Issues and What Makes Them Hot, Information Strategy: The Executive's Journal; Spring 2003, Vol. 19 Issue 3, p23, 14p.

Kotler, P. & Keller, K., (2006). Marketing Management. Pearson Education, Inc.: Upper Saddle River, NY: ISBN: 0-13-145757-8.

Lancaster, L.C. & Stillman, D. (2002). When generations collide: Who they are. Why they clash. How to solve the generational puzzle at work. New York, NY: HarperCollins Publishers Inc.

Laudon, K.C. & Laudon, J.P. (2007). Management information systems: Managing the digital firm. Upper Saddle River, NJ. Pearson Prentice Hall.

Marketing information systems practices in small manufacturing firms: Antecedents and consequences, Louis Raymond, Jacques Brisoux, Abdellah Azami. The Journal of Computer Information Systems. Stillwater: Spring 2001. Vol. 41, Iss. 3; pg. 32, 10 pgs.

Martinuzzi, Bruna, (2009). The Leader as a Mensch: Become the Kind of Person Others Want to Follow, San Francisco, CA. Intelligence Press.

McGrath, S. (2008, April) Defining success for IT projects, Retrieved May 10, 2008, from: http://www.itworld.com/Tech/4535/define-success-it-projects-nlstipsm-080415/index.html.

McShane, S. L., & Von Gilnow, M. A. (2008). Organizational behavior (4th ed.). New York: McGraw-Hill/Irwin.

Porter, Michael E., Competitive Advantage: Creating and Sustaining Superior Performance, The Free Press, New York, 1985.

Reuters Financial, Retrieved April 21, 2007, from http://stocks.us.reuters.com/stocks/incomeStatement.asp?WTmodLOC=C3-FindOut-3-FinancialStatements&period=Q.

Rheem, H. (1995) Effective Leadership: The Pygmalion Effect. Harvard Business Review, May/June, 1995, Vol. 73 Issue 3, p 14.

Robbins, G (2001, May) The Robbins-Gioia Survey (2001), Retrieved May 10, 2008, from http://www.it-cortex.com/home.htm.

Sheridan, B., (2011). Stars and Stripes And Servers Forever: Bloomberg Businessweek; February, 2011, p 33-35.

Surowiecki, James (2004). The Wisdom of Crowds: Why the Many Are Smarter Than the Few and How Collective Wisdom Shapes Business, Economies, Societies and Nations Little, Brown.

Thomas Davenport, Kathy Quirk. Competing on analytics. Optimize. Manhasset: Feb 2006. Vol. 5, Iss. 2; pg. 40, 7 pgs.

Thompson Jr A, Strickland III A, Gamble J. (2008). Crafting and executing strategy: The quest for competitive advantage: Concepts and cases. New York: McGraw-Hill.

W. J. Orlikowski and J. J. Baroudi (1991),"Studying Information Technology in Organisations: Research Approaches and Assumptions" *Information Systems Research*, Vol. 2, pp. 1-28.

Index

Index

Index

Index

Index

Index

T

V

W

X

Y

Z

Feedback

I am always interested in receiving comments from readers, especially business owners who have implemented or intend to implement the Anthead System in their organization. Please let him know of your progress.

Also, and this is a big one, please leave a review once you've had an opportunity to read the book. Potential readers tend to pay close attention to what previous readers have to say.

Please contact the author at:

adgrogan@antheadsystem.com

www.ingramcontent.com/pod-product-compliance
Lightning Source LLC
Chambersburg PA
CBHW060005210326
41520CB00009B/829